# The New
# Selling IQ

*Combining the Power
of Buyer-Seller Intelligence
to Optimize Results!*

*Kim D. Ward*

ISBN: 978-1-4834-5472-6 (sc)
ISBN: 978-1-4834-5471-9 (e)

Lulu Publishing Services rev. date: 7/27/2016

# Contents

# Foreword:

# Selling In The New Age

Generations have personalities. As each generation moves into their 20's and 30's they begin to reveal themselves as they act on their values, attitudes and world views. There is no doubt that Millennials are having an impact on the world as they incorporate their passions about issues, causes and beliefs into their busy, multifaceted lives. But what about the impact they are also having on buying, selling and the overall business landscape?

We all know that customer buying preferences have changed. Customers are less brand loyal, deluged with competing purchase choices, more environment and price sensitive while also maximizing internet channel marketing and other evolving technology resources and information. We also know that whether buying or selling millennials want to make a difference. As buyers they tend to look at the bigger picture, make more collaborative rather than independent decisions and desire buying decision guidance rather than sales pitches. As sellers, millennials prefer to offer consultative decision influence over canned presentations and closing techniques.

*To ignore these changing dynamics in people and the business environment in favor of sticking to traditional selling methodology makes little sense!*

As the CEO of **Learning Outsource Group** (*an internationally recognized provider of Sales and Sales Management training solutions*) I have been a close colleague and friend to Kim Ward for more than two decades. His dedication to helping clients to overcome work challenges, achieve performance goals and take their organizations to their next level are well known. As a respected thought leader in sales and sales leadership effectiveness, he has dedicated years of research to develop this sales methodology that I believe will change this and future business generations for the better.

I am convinced that **Cooperation Selling**™ is a much needed answer to the selling and buying pains our clients and their customers are experiencing. The merging of buyer and seller intelligence to create a collaborative and productive platform for today's sellers is brilliant! I challenge anyone to read this book and then walk away thinking that they want to sell the same old way. It will change your views on both buying and selling. But more importantly it will change sellers for the better!

Thomas Cooke

# Acknowledgements:

I would like to express my sincere gratitude to the thousands of professional sellers, leaders and clients whose willingness to openly share their experiences made the *Cooperation Selling* method and this book possible.

Thank you!

From The Author:

# Why Read This Book?

## The History of Selling Methodology

Over the years many experts have developed ideas resulting in unique variations of the traditional selling methodology. These included teaching sellers to focus more strategically on their customer accounts and the concept of selling value. Many of these methods have led to improved selling results.

And yet no matter how traditional selling is re-imagined, the foundation has always been focused on the *selling* process with little or no consideration for the customer's *buying* process. So the purpose of the traditional selling method has always been to sell by persuading customers to buy.

## Actions produce consequences!

As sellers have dedicated themselves to persuading customers to buy, their customers have naturally developed counterbalances. If the focus of one party is persuasion, then the focus of their intended target becomes resistance. To some degree this helps to explain why there are so many classes available on how to negotiate and purchase.

## To some degree customers really have changed!

As you may have already realized, today's customers are:

✓ Less trusting.
✓ More educated.
✓ Better informed.
✓ More price conscious.
✓ Better prepared.
✓ More demanding.

✓ Less patient.
✓ Inundated with competitive purchase choices.
✓ More likely to call on a seller only after they are well into their decision process.

So as we understand the changes in customer's perceptions and behavior and if true and sustainable improvement is going to be realized; then sellers and their leadership must recognize that polishing up the old way of selling is not the best way to get where they want to go.

## You can put fresh paint on an old house...but it is still an old house!

In order to truly change the way customers view and interact with sellers, more than a selling makeover is going to be required. The only way to effect this change is to completely retool the selling process. This involves creating a selling methodology which causes dramatic positive shifts in both seller behavior and, in turn, customer behavior.

In addition, this new selling methodology should keep up with the increasing speed of change occurring in businesses and also synchronize sellers with changing buyer preferences.

## Cooperation Selling™ is a revolutionary new selling methodology that is the best and easiest way to accomplish these objectives!

This book contains a profound compilation of buyer and seller intelligence. This intelligence is a merging of the most recent buyer research, comprehensive purchase decision studies and accumulated best practices from more than 70,000 successful sellers.

The *Cooperation Selling*™ methodology is based on buying decision science and will aid sellers in positively influencing and guiding customers throughout their entire purchase decision process. It has proven to be easy to understand and yet powerful when scaled to any selling situation.

*Cooperation Selling*™ explains how people and businesses make buying decisions and then models the selling methodology into a partnering framework so that you can begin to:

- Synchronize selling with your customer's buying process.
- Replace selling traditions that can hinder customer engagement with the selling values, strategies and behaviors which eliminate resistance and speed up the purchase decision.
- Sell more and in less time.
- Improve your customer's perceptions of value in you and what you offer.
- Reduce negotiation frequency and frustration.
- Improve customer loyalty and retention.
- Boost longer term revenue generation.
- Navigate decision influence groups and become a 'trusted advisor' with more decision influencers.
- Differentiate as a more readily accepted 'Customer Centric' selling professional.

If you are a professional seller and want to sell more, in less time and create more completely satisfied clients then you should read this book!

# Chapter One:

# The New Selling IQ!

# From the Customer's Perspective

For over 20 years, I have had the opportunity to interact with thousands of buyers. What I have learned is that most have specific expectations of their sellers. This has been confirmed by the most recent research *"Sales Excellence Research"* conducted by the *Chally Group*. The following are today's customers' top five "seller" expectations:

## 1. Understand my business.

Given the amount of available information, customers have very little patience for educating sellers about their industry and company. They will however, answer what they believe are relevant questions about their goals, concerns and culture.

Furthermore, customers do not want to answer questions such as "How well do you think this solution will work here?" Their gauge of whether the seller understands their needs is based on how well the sales representative can connect their proposed solution's applications to the client's goals and the needs of their company.

## 2. Design the right applications for me.

Customers no longer want to be told how they must change or adapt to fit the proposed solution. Instead, customers expect sellers to understand their specific needs, then design and offer a solution that is in closer alignment with their goals, processes and culture.

This doesn't necessarily mean that every solution sold must be a tailored one. But what it does mean is that if the product or solution cannot be tailored, then it must only be sold to those who believe that they are gaining the naturally ideal fit. This requires sellers to possess solid business acumen, connect with a broader range of prospects and ask more diagnostic questions. These things then lead to firmer customer qualification and satisfactory recommendations.

### 3. Treat me fairly and I'm more likely to trust you.

The bond of trust between the buyer and seller can be difficult to forge. Sellers must be a willing partner with their customers and have intentions of helping them to achieve their desired results.

Customers are less likely to offer their trust to a seller who does not appear to be reasonably concerned about them. They also expect the salesperson to provide them with reasonable and fair representation when liaising between the two companies.

Customers want to be treated openly and fairly. They want to know that sellers will conduct themselves with integrity when representing their products and services. Customers also want to know that sellers care enough about them to always try to do what is best for them. This does not mean that customers expect providers to sell without reasonable profit. What it means is that customers expect reasonable results and service when they have paid what they believe is a fair price for their purchase.

### 4. Be easily accessible to solve my problems should they occur.

Problems can occur even when a seller designs and sells the best possible solution. So if an issue does occur then customers expect sellers (and their support staff) to be available to help quickly and easily. Customers will no longer tolerate the "disappearing seller" without a suitable customer service channel that is readily accessible to solve their problem.

### 5.  Be creative when responding to my changing needs.

Everything is changing. What serves a customer well today may not be the same 3-6 months from now. And if we expand the scope of possible change over the coming year, how many additional changes might occur?

Developing fruitful relationships requires more than just helping customers one time and moving on. Great relationships are sustained by understanding that people, conditions and anything else can change. Being prepared and willing to continue helping customers in what could be very different ways as things change is paramount in continuing relationship development and partnering success.

# From the Seller's Perspective

During the last two plus decades I've had the privilege of working with tens of thousands of successful sellers, sales managers and leaders. Many of them had already achieved substantial success. And yet, because of the way things have changed almost all of them have had some level of concern about one or more of the following selling issues.

Their most common selling concerns have been how they might:

- Become more productive in initial prospect engagements.
- Achieve more selling productivity and in less time.

- Effectively communicate their competitive differentiators.
- Create greater and faster levels of perceived value in what they sell.
- Reduce the customer's price negotiation priority.
- Eliminate resistance in buyer-seller engagements.
- Broaden and deepen strategic alliances in current accounts.
- Improve overall customer loyalty.
- Effectively engage and win over behind the scenes decision influencers.
- Raise their selling profile with customers to create a true "Trusted Advisor" relationship.

From my observations, the best sellers effectively manage these concerns through the application of intelligence, introspection, asking influential questions and understanding the customer's decision making process. Let's examine each of these in more detail.

## Intelligence: *Information is power when selling!*

Great sellers:

- Pay attention to what is going on around them. They understand that change is the primary catalyst for growth.
- Know that understanding and working with change is necessary if they intend to grow and improve.
- Constantly gather information or "Intelligence" that will aid them in optimizing their selling efforts.
- Seek, interpret and leverage buyer intelligence with the hopes of better understanding their customers and improving selling results.

## Introspection: *The most powerful and positive personal developmental tool that sellers possess!*

Great sellers perpetually perform "checkups from the neck up" to promote the consistent improvement of their abilities and continued selling success. The best sellers are continuously asking themselves questions like:

- ✓ Do I know enough about what I'm selling and how it may benefit my customers?
- ✓ How well do I know my customers and what else do I need to know?
- ✓ Do I know enough about my competition to competitively differentiate?
- ✓ What can or should I change in order to improve my ability to sell and succeed?
- ✓ What should I start doing, stop doing or continue doing that will improve my chances of becoming even more successful?

The introspection that occurs in response to these questions drives great seller's efforts to continuously improve.

## Influence: *Everyone can be influenced by someone!*

Great sellers know that no matter how much they might sometimes wish that they could, they can't "make" customers buy. They also know that if they are going to influence a customer's purchasing decision then it will be accomplished with:

- Effective diagnostic questioning.
- Providing the customer with timely, relevant and useful information.

And, what great sellers understand most about influence is that it isn't something they 'do to' customers. It is something that is "allowed by" customers.

Whether or not a seller positively influences a customer's purchase decision is a choice that the customer will make. Customers decide whether or not to respect and trust a seller's suggestions and recommendations based on:

- ✓ Customer perception of the seller's credibility.
- ✓ Customer interpretation of the seller's intentions and behavior.
- ✓ Customer personal motivations to purchase.
- ✓ Customer perceptions of the need and viability of the proposed product or service.

## Influence Questions (IQ): *The greatest sellers are not those who know all of the answers but instead those who know all of the right questions!*

Customers want sellers to reasonably understand their industry and business before making contact. As one decision maker put it, "I don't want to waste my time answering questions that I believe should have been answered elsewhere." By asking the right questions, the best sellers influence the outcome of the purchase decision.

*Great sellers know that customers more frequently award their business to the seller who has partnered with them and guided them through their whole decision process.*

The most effective sellers use Influence Questions (IQ). Influence questions are those that gain the seller relevant information as well as help guide the customer through the decision making process.

Far too many sellers enter their selling engagements with little or no prepared selling plan. The best sellers proactively prepare to assist and guide customers through their entire decision process. By doing so, they find it much easier to influence and motivate their customers, and they do this with less customer resistance and more overall selling success!

# Leveraging Buyer and Seller Intelligence

Buying Decision Science: *Effective selling has very little to do with selling. Selling should begin with understanding buying!*

Understanding the *Buying Decision Science* creates predictability with purchase decisions. It explains what customers are thinking about as they move through their purchase decision process. The most effective sellers are able to:

- Identify who is involved in the decision making process.
- Determine the role each decision influencer plays in the decision process.
- Proactively prepare to help their customers in asking and answering their internal questions which drive the buying decision.

The *Cooperation Selling*™ *"Influence Questions"* are used to pro-actively prepare sellers for their selling engagements. By under-standing the buying decision science and proactively preparing to positively influence the customer by proactively using *Influence Questions (IQ's)*, great sellers sell more, in less time and with more customer collaboration.

## Are Buyers and Sellers Talking About the Same Things?

It is interesting to compare what the customers are seeking to what the best sales people are doing. There are a number of matches that include understanding the customer's business and asking the right questions at the right time in order to positively influence the decision making process.

In the next chapters, we are going to explore how to bring you, and ultimately your customer, to a new level: A level of coop-eration in which you can both achieve your results.

# Cooperation Selling™ Core Values

According to psychologists, the way we think influences the way we feel. And the way we feel influences the way we behave. As a seller it is important to make sure that you possess the right attitudes about your customers and your role as a seller in order to make it as easy as possible for your customers to buy from you. This starts with some simple recommendations of attitude.

The *Cooperation Selling*™ recommendations and suggestions:

1.  Understand that customers are people who are simply try-ing to do what is best and that they may not have always had good previous experiences with sellers.

2. Just because selling and buying has been previously viewed as an adversarial relationship doesn't mean that this perception, attitude, and behavior must continue.
3. The way we think and feel has impact and encourages our behavior as people and as sellers.
4. A seller's true role is to guide the customer toward making their best decision.
5. A seller's purpose is to find ways to help the customer improve their condition or situation by recommending the right products and services.

In addition, the Cooperation Selling™ - Core Values are suggested as guiding principles for achieving the greatest selling and relationship returns. If the way we think and feel influences the way we behave, then embracing and adopting these core values will produce the best possible partnering and selling outcomes.

Here is an overview of the *Cooperation Selling™* - Core Values. In the *Resource Guide: Initiating Cooperation Selling™*, we will cover each of these in-depth as well as strategies for integrating them into your daily selling efforts.

1. *Approach with helping intentions.*
2. *Change the customer's experience.*
3. *Demonstrate honesty and credibility.*
4. *Ask and listen.*
5. *Be open minded.*
6. *Create an environment of support.*
7. *Know everything about your solution.*
8. *Expect cooperative partnerships.*

As each Core Value is internalized, the seller's ultimate relationships with customers will be made more rewarding, yield more sales and last longer.

Chapter Two:

# Breaking The Code: The Science of Decision Making

# The Science of Decision Making

People make decisions every day. Some decisions are given deeper consideration than others. For example, most people don't dwell on their choice of socks in the morning. On the other hand, the same can't be said when they purchase a new home.

The decisions that people invest in most are the ones in which they feel they have the most to win or lose when making them. Additionally, when making these riskier decisions people tend to take a more rational decision process approach. This can lessen decision maker anxiety and may improve the decision outcome. This is especially true when making consequential buying decisions.

*As the perception of risk and anxiety increases so does the decision maker's need for a rational and quantifiable decision process!*

What raises a buyer's sense of risk? Any one of the following can contribute to the perceived risk and associated anxiety:

- Over Spending: *Where can I get the best price for this?*
- Not Receiving the Desired Benefits: *Will this do what it is supposed to do?*
- Wasting Time: *Am I overthinking this?*
- Loss of Personal or Business Reputation: *If I make a bad decision, what are the ramifications?*
- Product Obsolescence: *Should I wait for the next version to come out?*
- Change: *Should we just stay with what we have now?*
- The Disapproval of Others: *What if the others don't like this?*
- Integration Concerns: *How easily will it fit into our existing systems, procedures and culture?*

- Repeating Poor Past Experiences: *I made a bad decision the last time.*
- Not Receiving the Expected or Desired Value: *Will this be worth what I spend?*

# The Buying Decision Process

People don't really want to make decision mistakes, particularly when making large, less frequent, but riskier purchase decisions. So they attempt to improve their chances of making a more successful decision by using a very common and rational decision process. They use a *Buying Decision Process* which gives them a feeling of control and direction when making purchase decisions.

*A Buying Decision Process is a series of actions which hopefully lead to a more productive decision.*

These actions become a series of steps which the buyer believes will lead to the best decision. However, the process begins with a question about motivation:

*Is making this decision important to me?*

As buyers perceive a greater sense of decision risk concerning things like responsibility, purchased applications, decision implications and other possible consequences, they engage in what they believe will be a safer and more rational decision process.

However, too much perceived risk can become decision debilitating and stop forward movement in the decision process altogether.

*If the perceived risk becomes greater than the anticipated benefits, the decision may be postponed or avoided altogether!*

Think back to the last major purchase you considered and then avoided. Now ask yourself, "What caused me to abandon that purchase?" In most cases, the perceived risk was greater than the benefit you hoped to achieve from that purchase.

If a person's concerns or perceived risks are ever greater than their motivation for making the decision, then they are far more likely to remain status quo or do nothing at all.

*Your customers may not even realize they are using a Buying Decision Process.*

The Buying Decision Process occurs whether the buyer realizes that they are using a defined, rational process or not. But whether or not the buyer realizes that they are doing it doesn't change the fact that it is happening. Additionally, whether they do or don't realize they are using a process, a seller's role remains the same.

*Effective selling begins when the seller aligns with the buyer in their decision process.*

So how do we "align" with the buyer? It begins with understanding how people buy and then using appropriate and effective strategies to support and guide them through their buying experience. Those strategies include:

## STRATEGY: Recognizing that the greater the risk, the more quantifiable the solution may need to be.

Because the customer perceives more risk in making a decision, he or she will probably demand more quantifiable answers to their questions. And, the more quantifiable the customer's internal questions become the more tangible the answers must become. So the more decision risk the customer perceives the more sellers should help them with quantifiable answers to their questions.

## STRATEGY: Accurately identifying where the customer is in the Buying Decision Process.

Because the buyer doesn't want to make a decision mistake they use a decision process which is predictable. This predictability allows sellers to identify where the customer is in their process then apply influence strategies that are appropriate to that decision step.

## STRATEGY: Guiding the customer's decision by applying Influence Questions (IQ's).

Once sellers have determined where their customer is in the Buying Decision Process, they should partner with them and guide them. By proactively applying their Influence Questions (IQ's) sellers are best prepared to suggest the questions that customers should be asking and identify the quantifiable information they are seeking during their purchase decision process.

# Buying Decision: Process Steps and Internal Questions

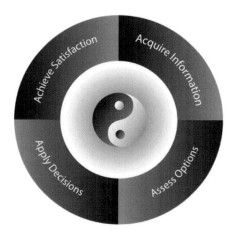

The common customer *Buying Decision Process* consists of four steps. Each step has an associated goal.

- ✓ Acquire Information
  *(Decision Step Goal: Determining whether a decision is important and needed)*

- ✓ Assess Options
  *(Decision Step Goal: Determining what is needed, wanted and available)*

- ✓ Apply Decisions
  *(Decision Step Goal: Determining and choosing the best possible decision element options)*

- ✓ Achieve Satisfaction
  *(Decision Step Goal: Determining whether the purchase outcomes and results are as hoped and expected)*

In each customer buying decision step customers ask and answer *Internal Questions* that help them determine whether they are on the best decision path and have the motivation to continue forward in their decision process. By asking and answering these Internal Questions in each buying decision step, decision makers avoid making decision mistakes and cause their decision process to become more rational and quantifiable.

In the next chapter we will view the Buying Decision Process and associated Internal Questions in depth. For now, let's just take a cursory look the buying decision process steps and the related list of decision maker's internal questions.

# Buying Decision Process Steps and Internal Questions

| *Buying Decision Steps* | *Decision Maker Internal Questions* |
| --- | --- |
| Acquire Information | ✓ Is making this decision important to me?<br>✓ Which sources of information do I trust?<br>✓ What could it cost me to make or not make this decision? |
| Assess Options | ✓ How many possible decision choices are available and which one is best for me?<br>✓ What questions do I need answered before I can move forward with my decision?<br>✓ Do I still perceive enough value to proceed forward with my decision? |

| Buying Decision Steps | Decision Maker Internal Questions |
|---|---|
| Apply Decisions | ✓ Am I still comfortable with my decision criterion?<br>✓ Have I considered all of the available decision options and chosen the one that is best for me?<br>✓ Do I still perceive enough value in making the decision? |
| Achieve Satisfaction | ✓ Am I achieving the results I expected?<br>✓ Have my expectations changed?<br>✓ Will I continue to do business with the provider company? |

# Customer Decision Step – Common Decision Step Indicators

*Where is the customer in their buying decision process?*

Sellers can easily determine where customers are in their decision process by paying close attention to the customer's behavior, questions they ask and the conversation they offer. Just remember that the customer's behaviors, questions and conversation are ordinarily a byproduct of the Internal Questions that they are attempting to ask and answer as they move through their Buying Decision Process.

The following is a chart reflecting the *Buying Decision Steps*, the buyer's *Internal Questions* and the most common *Decision Step Indicators* which sellers can use to identify where the buyer is in their decision process.

| Customer Buying Decision Steps | Common Decision Step Indicators |
|---|---|
| **Acquire Information** | |
| ✓ Is making this decision important to me? <br> ✓ Which sources of information do I trust? <br> ✓ What could it cost me to make or not make this decision? | • Wants initial information to determine situation <br> • Willing to do some preliminary research <br> • Unsure about what is needed or wanted <br> • Talks about previous bad buying experiences <br> • Willing to talk; but hesitant to give any relevant information or commitments |
| **Assess Options** | |
| ✓ How many possible decision choices are available and which one is best for me? <br> ✓ What questions do I need answered before I can move forward with my decision? <br> ✓ Do I still perceive enough value to proceed forward with my decision? | • Has yet to settle into making the decision <br> • Seems to still be gathering information from multiple sources <br> • Has not decided exactly what they want to do <br> • Shows concern for not knowing enough <br> • Asks questions about price or shopping price before deciding what they want or want to do |
| **Apply Decisions** | |
| ✓ Am I still comfortable with my decision criterion? <br> ✓ Have I considered all of the available decision options and chosen the one that is best for me? <br> ✓ Do I still perceive enough value in making the decision? | • Perceives possible decision risk to be greater than current perceived value <br> • Ready to move forward but wants to negotiate <br> • Talks about others they must satisfy with the decision <br> • Starts asking about implementation or terms <br> • Suggests what they want or need going forward |

| Customer Buying Decision Steps | Common Decision Step Indicators |
|---|---|
| *Achieve Satisfaction* | |
| ✓ Am I achieving the results I expected?<br>✓ Have my expectations changed?<br>✓ Will I continue to do business with the provider company? | • Happy or unhappy with solution performance<br>• Suggests that there are other criteria or people that should have been considered<br>• Seems to be measuring service capabilities, experience and performance<br>• Will or will not give reference or referral |

Keep the following in mind:

*Customers are far more likely to buy from salespeople who understand, align with and help them through their buying decision process!*

Chapter Three:

# Buying Decision
# Process Steps

# A Deeper Dive into The Science of Buying

*Customers are far more likely to award their business to the seller who has accompanied them through their entire buying decision process!*

Customers are far more likely to award their business to the seller who understands how they make decisions and then becomes a guiding partner in their process. Also, focusing on the customer and their decision process and then assisting them in making their best decisions creates levels of trust and appreciation that cannot be accomplished by any other means.

In order to better understand what customers are thinking and the goals they hope to accomplish with their Buying Decision Process let's examine each of the common customer buying decision steps more closely.

# Buying Decision Process Step One: Acquire Information

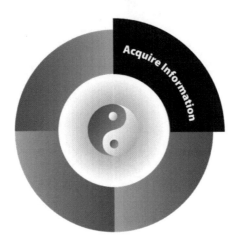

## Acquire Information Internal Questions

- Is making this decision important to me?
- Which sources of information do I trust?
- What could it cost me to make or not make this decision?

The first Buying Decision Process step is *Acquire Information*. In this step the customers are determining:

- Whether any effort should be expended making a purchase decision.
- The sources of information that they feel comfortable using.
- The possible costs associated with not making a decision and instead remaining status quo.

Customers ask themselves three important Internal Questions to determine if they are motivated to consider making a purchase decision. Let's look more closely at their internal questions.

# Acquire Information - Internal Questions

As was mentioned in the previous chapter, in each of the four steps of the customer Buying Decision Process there are three principal Internal Questions which the customer will ask of themselves and answer. In the *Acquire Information* decision step the following is the first of these three questions.

- Is making this decision important to me?

A person's priorities drive their decisions which result in their actions. By asking this internal question the decision maker wants to determine whether they consider the decision to be a priority. If their answer to the first internal question is "no" then their buying process usually stops. If this should occur in the initial conversation with a seller, then the decision maker has little or no motivation to continue.

On the other hand, if the salesperson offers motivational reasoning which causes the customer to see value in moving forward in the decision process, then the decision maker will begin processing the second internal question in the Acquire Information decision step. Most sellers have been taught to offer or suggest some statements of value when they approach and initially engage a prospect. They do this in the hope that the value they suggest will be recognized and appreciated by the prospect. An example of this *is:*

*"We help customers improve productivity while reducing overall costs!"*

If the prospect has an appreciation for either increasing productivity or reducing costs they may choose to engage further with the seller. If that is not a priority, the Buying Decision Process may stop at that point.

- ## Which sources of information do I trust?

There was a time when sellers were their customer's primary source of information when making buying decisions. Today the number one decision making information resource is the internet. In fact, because the internet is so easily accessible, sellers have become some of the last resources that decision makers choose to use. And yet accessibility is not the only reason that decision makers go to the internet for information, it's also an issue of trust.

Some sellers have driven decision makers to look for what they believe are more trustworthy sources of information. Some stereotypical selling behaviors have caused decision makers to believe that many sellers are acting in their own self-interest. Given that, customers may not readily trust sellers.

Once the customer determines which information sources they trust, then they begin to review, analyze and consider the information they've acquired. Now they can ask and answer the next internal question in their *Acquire Information* decision step:

- ## What could it cost me to make or not make this decision?

Determining reasonable cause for making a purchase decision is the customer act of determining whether they perceive enough initial value to move forward with their purchase decision.

When a customer internally asks *"What could it cost me to make or not make this decision?"* they are weighing the potential benefits of making the decision against their estimated cost of *not* making the decision.

## Value Equation

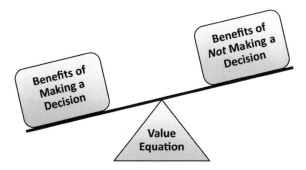

If the benefits of making the decision outweigh the risk or cost of <u>not</u> making the decision, then the Buying Decision Process will continue. Often this occurs when the sales representative has presented proposed value in the initial conversation that is relevant to the customer's situation. So in this case the customer believes that there is more value in moving forward with their decision than doing nothing or simply maintaining the "status quo."

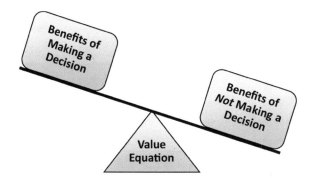

However, if the customer determines that the benefits of *not* making a decision *(or taking no action)* outweigh the benefits of making a decision, then the Buying Decision Process will probably cease.

Once the customer has completed their first buying decision step of *Acquire Information* and they feel there is reasonable and motivational cause to continue forward with their Buying Decision Process, then they rationally progress to their next decision step, Assess Options.

# Assess Options - Internal Questions

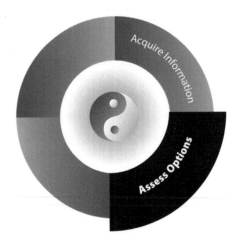

## Assess Options Internal Questions

- How many possible decision choices are available and which one is best for me?
- What questions do I need answered before I can move forward with my decision?
- Do I still perceive enough value to proceed forward with making the decision?

Once the decision maker recognizes enough initial value and motivation from asking and answering their *Acquire Information* internal questions then they continue forward with their next purchase decision step called *Assess Options*.

In the *Assess Options* decision step, customers also ask themselves three Internal Questions. The first of these is:

- How many possible decision choices are available and which one is best for me?

Before a customer makes a purchase decision they must first determine what they want or need to accomplish with their purchase. These determined desires or expectations are commonly called "Buying Decision Criteria." Decision criteria are what decision makers use to compare purchase choice options so they can make their final purchase selection.

Decision makers create their list of decision criteria by:

- ✓ Considering or analyzing their current situation or condition.
- ✓ Determining any gap between the current situation and their perception of an optimal condition.
- ✓ Researching possible products, services or solutions to determine what they really want and need.

Developing specific decision criteria helps the customer to review their possible choices and select the one that they believe will be best for them. Some decision makers begin by creating a list of specifications, budgets and the dates in which the solution will be implemented.

More often, decision makers do their research by looking at possible options on the internet. Those options help them craft the buying criteria but in doing so they bypass one of the most valuable resources for obtaining purchase decision information; the seller.

Uncovering a prospect that has not yet started the decision process is one of the best ways to influence the buying criteria. When a seller brings up improvement opportunities, the decision makers may begin a purchase decision process which otherwise may not have been considered. At that point the seller:

- Is involved before any competitor.
- Can most easily influence the buying decision criteria.
- Stands the best chance of becoming a trusted information resource.

As decision makers do research to uncover information about options, they can develop additional decision criteria which they had not previously considered. Because of the additional information decision makers uncover they are usually prompted to ask the second internal question in the *Assess Options* decision step. This second Internal Question is:

- **What questions do I need answered before I can move forward with my decision?**

There are several motives which can drive this Internal Question, but the two most common motives are:

1. A robust selection of possible purchase choices.
2. Uncovered information which spurs decision criteria which have not been previously considered.

It's easy to understand how several options or choices can raise additional questions for decision makers. Consider your last technology decision such as a phone or tablet. You probably realized very quickly that there are a multitude of choice options. The more options you considered, the more possible questions of differentiation, application and value probably occurred. For you to have felt comfortable in your purchase, these questions had to be answered to your satisfaction.

## The Options, Questions, Confidence Connection

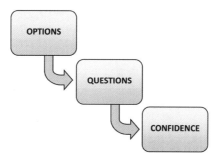

As the decision maker discovers more options, they ask more questions about those options. The answers to those questions directly impact the degree of confidence your customer has in making the right decision. Given that, the more options that are available, the more questions the customer is likely to ask.

Remember that in the Acquire Information step one of the customer's internal questions is, "Which sources of information do I trust?"

## *Those who proactively ask and answer valid questions gain the customer's confidence!*

As the seller exposes the customer to more options, the customer develops more questions. Some of these are spoken but many are not. The most effective sellers are those who not only present the options but proactively answer the questions that might be in the customer's mind.

How do you know what those questions might be? Simply reflect back on conversations you have had with your other customers. The questions some have verbalized are probably the same questions others are asking themselves but not articulating.

Once decision makers have gained enough confidence from having their questions answered, then they will ask themselves the third and final internal question in the *Assess Options* decision step:

- Do I still perceive enough value to move forward with making the decision?

At this point decision makers do another cursory examination of what they know so far and decide if they have enough motivation to continue forward in their decision process.

In their first step *Acquire Information* decision makers are asking, *"What could it cost me to make or not make this decision?"* But after gaining a more in depth understanding of what they want or need and the choice options which might be available, then they will ask themselves another motivation question, *"Do I still perceive enough value in making the decision?"*

The two questions are similar because they both require the decision maker to consider the value equation. If the customer still perceives enough value in making the purchase decision then they move forward in their Buying Decision Process and, if not, then the purchase decision may be postponed or even abandoned.

*New information can raise additional customer questions which can either speed up or slow down the decision process!*

Consider our model again but note that there is a new arrow.

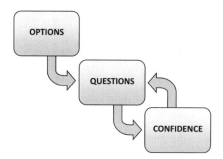

If you answer your customer's questions effectively, their decision confidence will grow. Less than effective answers to their questions will not only lower that confidence, it will cause them to ask *even more* questions. So consider that more questions can, at times, be an indicator of your customer's confidence level. If the confidence level gets too low, the purchase decision can be abandoned.

This is why it is so important for sellers to understand all of the internal questions that customers will be asking themselves as they move through their Buying Decision Process. Further, the seller must be able to respond to these questions in such a way that it boosts the customer's confidence.

Keep in mind that at times, the answers to the questions open a host of new options for the customer to consider. When that occurs, sellers must help them connect these options to the possible future value these newly discovered options may provide. Customers may not be able to do that on their own. So by guiding customers through this, sellers stand a much better chance of speeding up the decision process and become the customer's provider of choice. Sellers who cannot do this may find that they have simply complicated the customer's decision and inadvertently caused the decision process to stall or discontinue.

When the customer is reasonably comfortable with their purchase decision criteria and if they believe there will be enough future value created by the purchase then they will continue to the Apply *Decisions* decision step.

# Apply Decisions - Internal Questions

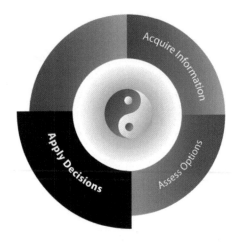

## Apply Decisions Internal Questions

- Am I still comfortable with my decision criteria?
- Have I considered all of the decision options and chosen the one that is best for me?
- Do I still perceive enough value to move forward with my decision?

In the *Apply Decisions* buying decision step decision makers compare available decision options against their decision criteria. Customers use this final check to determine whether they are making the best possible purchase choice. If they believe that there is a good pairing between their decision criteria and the proposed purchase and if they still possess enough motivation to buy then they will complete the purchase.

Once again, there are three commonly asked and answered internal questions as customers move through their *Apply Decisions* step. The first of these three questions is:

- Am I still comfortable with my decision criteria?

Decision makers want to feel comfortable with the decision criteria they've developed so they continually compare their criteria to the proposed purchase in order to make the best possible choices. This can also be escalated by the need to incorporate the decision criteria of several influencers in order to satisfy all of their needs. Another reason for this "double checking" is that the decision maker may have made what they considered to be some poor purchasing decisions in the past and hope to avoid doing so again.

- Have I considered all of the available decision options and chosen the one that is best for me?

Making a purchase decision when multiple choices exist almost always includes the customer doing some comparisons. In order to narrow their field of choices customers compare their predetermined and prioritized decision criteria against the choices available so they can determine which one they believe is the best overall fit. Most likely, the customer will choose to purchase the product that aligns most closely with their decision criteria and their priorities for those criteria. This is called the Criteria-to-Solution Alignment.

When considering this in context with the rest of the Buying Decision Process, this is a relatively simple portion of the process to understand. The decision maker is attempting to determine which purchase choice best matches their decision criteria and priorities.

## When salespeople lose a sale to the competition and don't understand why they commonly assume it was because of price!

Sellers don't always seem to understand what actually occurs when a customer is attempting to answer their second *Apply Decisions question*. This is proven true almost every time a seller loses a sale to their competitor and they don't understand why. Many sellers will say they lost the sale because of price. But in reality it is almost always because the seller's solution did not align with the customer's buying criteria. So how do you create a situation where the Criteria-to-Solution Alignment works in your favor?

First, work with the customer early in the Buying Decision Process to help define buying criteria that:

- More closely aligns your offering with the customer's decision criteria and priorities.
- Eliminates competitive choices in favor of your better aligned recommendations.

Once this is done, then walk the customer through the similarities between your solution and their agreed upon buying criteria.

Once the decision maker feels that they have settled on a purchase decision choice which is in close enough alignment to their decision criteria and priorities then their next natural internal question comes to mind:

- *Do I still perceive enough value in making the decision?*

This buyer internal question can slow down or even derail more purchase decisions than any other. When a purchasing decision which appears to be moving forward dries up and the sale disappears it is most frequently due to the decision maker not being able to affirmatively answer this question.

*If the perceived cost (pain) ever becomes greater than the perceived value (motivation) then the customer may completely abandon the decision process!*

Many sellers still don't do a very good job of guiding customers to positively answer this internal question. As a result, the decision maker may not perceive enough value when comparing it in the balance with perceived cost and as a result their decision stops moving forward. In fact, the decision process can actually begin to go backward. Consider this:

This internal question, *"Do I still perceive enough value in making the decision?"* is like a decision "fail safe" that buyers have unconsciously built into their decision process. It's the angel on their shoulder who whispers, *"Hey… you may not want to do that!"* It's the voice in their head that says, *"You know what? You don't have to do this right now!"* It's the most common cause of going backwards in a decision process.

If the seller hasn't helped the decision maker to discover compelling value through the creation of decision making criteria and solution alignment, then it is probably too late to do so now. (In fact, many initial decision maker perceptions of decision value are created much earlier in the *Acquire Information* buying decision step.)

*Sales are commonly lost late in the decision process because customers do not possess enough motivating "cause" for completing the purchase decision!*

Salespeople who focus on selling rather than the customer decision process seem to run into this situation quite frequently. It happens because they allowed or encouraged the customer to move too quickly past their first and sometimes second decision steps. The result can be that the customer doesn't perceive enough value to complete their purchase. This is also most frequently where objections and negotiations occur. We'll discuss managing and overcoming both logical and emotional customer objections later, but it is much easier to proactively prevent these objections than it is to handle them when they occur this late in the decision process.

## Achieve Satisfaction - Internal Questions

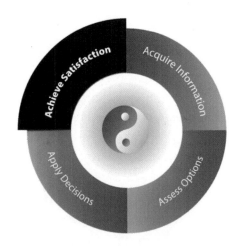

## Achieve Satisfaction Internal Questions

- Am I achieving the results I expected?
- Have my expectations changed?
- Will I continue to do business with the provider company?

## *The customer's purchase may be completed... but their decision process continues!*

The Buying Decision Process continues after the actual purchase to the fourth customer decision step which is *Achieve Satisfaction*. Sellers have not always viewed the after purchase internal questioning that customers go through to be part of the customer decision process. Ergo, traditional selling procedures rarely included after purchase decision strategies for guiding customers through this step of their decision process. But now with the help of the buying decision science sellers can become more consistently prepared to:

- ✓ Increase levels of customer and decision satisfaction.
- ✓ Improve their relationships with customers.
- ✓ Maintain completely satisfied customers longer.

If a customer is left to their own devices and not guided by the seller through their final buying decision process step, the likelihood of forming a meaningful and lasting bond between the seller and customer almost disappear. So what are customers asking themselves once they've made their final purchase decision? The customer's Achieve Satisfaction internal questions start with:

- *Am I achieving the results I expected?*

At some point after most customers complete their purchase they begin expecting the results they envisioned achieving.

## Undefined expectations lead to dissatisfying results!

Satisfaction is the hope of almost every customer at the time of purchase. And yet, far too many are ultimately unsatisfied. When customers ask themselves, *"Am I achieving the results I expected?"* what they are really attempting to discern is, "Are my decision criteria being effectively fulfilled in a reasonable and expected time frame?"

If a customer begins to think that their purchase is not satisfying them then they will be most likely satisfied with themselves but less than satisfied with the provider. They may even choose to believe that the provider should have helped them make better choices. In other words, "I made the best decision I could with the information the seller gave me. The outcome would have been better had he done a better job."

Sellers need to understand that when customer dissatisfaction occurs after the sale, a big part of the cause is poorly defined:

- Buying Criteria: *The customer did not consider all of needs or applications for this product.*
- Implementation Expectations: *The customer did not anticipate challenges associated with the installation of the product.*
- Long-Term Results: *The customer expected more from the solution than it was capable of delivering.*

Sellers can proactively address all three of these and increase the chances of having a highly satisfied customer.

## STRATEGY: Dig deeper to uncover all of the possible decision criteria

In many cases, the customer blames the seller if the solution doesn't meet their needs. This can be caused by not helping the customer uncover all of their possible decision criteria during the earlier steps of the buying process. All the customer knows is that they are unsatisfied with their purchase at that moment and the seller should have been of more help. Sellers who move too soon to offer recommendations without uncovering all of the customer's decision criteria tend to create customer dissatisfaction.

## STRATEGY: Help manage customer implementation expectations

The more sellers manage the customer's expectations of solution implementation, the higher the degree of satisfaction. The customer may expect delivery sooner, easy implementation and their results immediately achieved. Many sellers are reluctant to discuss these with the customer for fear of endangering the sale. The reality is that by carefully explaining all of the aspects of the implementation of the solution, the customer will usually have more realistic expectations that can then be met or exceeded.

## STRATEGY: Clarify short and long term expectations

Depending upon what the customer purchased they may be expecting immediate results or R.O.I. If solution results take time then the seller who manages the expectations of when purchase payback will occur will have the highest level of customer satisfaction.

And then, sometimes things just change. Because change does occur, customers in the *Achieve Satisfaction* step of the customer Buying Decision Process ask themselves the next internal question:

- *Have my expectations changed?*

Let's face it, the "new, bright and shiny" wears off of some purchases very quickly. After a relatively short purchase decision honeymoon, the customer will decide whether their purchase and provider are still meeting their continued and sometimes changing expectations for satisfaction.

Whether customers experience initial purchase satisfaction or not, at some point they will ask themselves, "Have my expectations changed?" And, as a customer implements and uses their purchase they hope to achieve not just value but "extended value."

## Extended Value is created from continued customer satisfaction as things change.

So the internal question, "Have my expectations changed?" is normally prompted by the customer identifying a new need that they want their purchase to fulfill. There are a number of common after purchase "need" producing drivers. Some of these need drivers are things like:

A. Application needs
B. Utilization needs
C. Business or responsibility growth
D. The need for new or improved results
E. New information
F. New technology or technology advances
G. New users
H. Loss of trust or confidence
I. Increased costs
J. Service needs

These need drivers are the most common catalysts causing customers to re-evaluate their perceptions of satisfaction after the initial implementation evaluation has been completed. This commonly occurs because of one or more changes have been identified.

How can the seller minimize dissatisfaction when things change? It begins with helping the customer think in the long-term when establishing their buying criteria. Are they considering the drivers shown above? Sellers should also stay in touch with their customers throughout their implementations of the solution and beyond.

## *People who care communicate! Stay in contact... a lot!*

In many companies, once the sale is made the implementation and even customer service is handed over to others. The theory is that the sales representative is then free to pursue new sales. While this can be an effective strategy, it can also cause the seller to not be aware of changing conditions that might lead to dissatisfaction. Keep in mind that the customer can be satisfied with the product but not with the provider. In many cases, the first the seller may find out about this dissatisfaction is when things have gone horribly wrong and the customer calls or completes an unhappy evaluation. In either case, it may be too late to turn the situation around.

By staying in touch with your customer, you increase the likelihood of the greatest satisfaction. From that grows positive evaluations, referrals and the possibility of future sales with this customer.

Staying in contact with a customer can mean a healthy mix of visits, phone calls, emails and formal evaluations. Most formal evaluations ask questions like, "Would you recommend your purchase or us to others?" or "Would you be willing to be a reference?"

These questions cause the customer to consider the last internal question in their *Achieve Satisfaction* buying decision step.

- *Will I continue to do business with the provider company?*

This internal question will come to mind when the customer feels that answering the question is a priority. The question can become a priority for the customer if one or more of the following situations occur:

- ✓ There is a possible need for additional purchases.
- ✓ There is a request for a survey, reference or introduction.
- ✓ Someone (or a survey) asks the customer for an opinion about the purchase or provider.

In any of these situations the customer will ask the internal question, *"Will I continue to do business with the provider company?"* The answer to this question will for the most part be based on their answers to several "sub-questions:"

- Was I satisfied with this last purchase and the provider?
- Were my decision criteria met or exceeded?
- Do I feel that the last purchase will continue to deliver value in the future?

The answers to these questions will influence the degree to which the customer is "completely satisfied."

*Great references, referrals and introductions become more likely as the customer has "completely satisfied" experiences!*

So if the customer affirms that they are willing to do business with the provider again then they will offer positive comments, references and introductions. Plus, it becomes very likely that the customer will view the seller and their company as their "Provider of Choice" when they are ready to consider their next purchase.

# The Next Purchase Decision

*Now, the Buying Decision Process can begin again!*

In our previous review of "value" creation *(refer to Customer Decision Step One: Acquire Information)* initial decision value is either perceived or not by the customer asking and answering the question, *"What will it cost me to make or not make this decision?"* The next buying decision for the same or a similar purchase will begin in the same way. The customer must determine if they have motivational cause for making another purchase decision. It is as if the customer has come full circle with their decision process.

## Buying Decision Process

The really good news for sellers who create enough customer satisfaction is:

## *Previous customer satisfaction can speed up the next purchase decision process!*

The customer started their first Buying Decision Process with *Acquire Information* and asked and answered three internal questions:

1. Is making the decision important to me?
2. What sources of information do I trust?
3. What would it cost me to make or not make this decision?

Now that the customer is ready to begin their next purchase decision and since they have experienced previous satisfaction, then the first two internal questions become much easier for them to answer and the process happens more quickly.

An example of this is when a seller brings new information about a recently upgraded product to their customer for consideration. If the customer has a need for another purchase and has some initial decision motivation to do so, then they will ask:

*"Is making this decision important to me?"*

With the experience of previous satisfaction, customers tend to assign more credibility to the seller and their suggestions in turn speeding up the answer to their first new purchase decision question.

*"What sources of information do I trust?"*

This same level of credibility and trust are also positive influences for the customer's second internal question. If the customer has had an excellent first experience, then the seller's recommendations are held in higher regard. In some circumstances, the customer may not even consider another source.

*"Will I continue to do business with the provider company?"*

If answered affirmatively, decision makers tend to move quickly through the first two internal questions in the Acquire Information buying decision step. This takes them almost immediately to the internal question, "What will it cost me to make or not make this decision?" and if they perceive initial decision value then the next purchase decision process begins.

# Chapter Four:

# Combining The Power of Buyer and Seller Intelligence

# Cooperation Selling (IQ) Foundation

*The goal of Cooperation Selling™ is to harmonize the intentions, motivations and actions of the provider and customer!*

Now that we understand the process customer's use for making purchase decisions, let's consider how sellers can accompany and guide them through their whole decision process. We know what customers want. They want to do what they prefer and believe is best for them.

We also know that:

- The greater a person's sense of risk and anxiety when decision making, the more rational and quantifiable the decision process becomes.
- Rationality in the decision process creates predictability!

Recognizing and understanding the rational process that people use when making significant purchase decisions allows us to begin looking at selling in a whole new way. We can help to minimize the customer's sense of risk and relieve their anxiety.

Rather than viewing selling as something which sellers do *to* customers, Cooperation Selling™ is something that sellers do *with* customers as they accompany and guide them through their buying decision process. This is how true buyer/seller partnerships are created.

# Partnering Begins with Decision Leveraging

*Decision leveraging is proactive seller preparation which enhances the exchange of information between the seller and their customer!*

Cooperation Selling™ uses Decision Leveraging to harmonize the relationship and communications between the provider and customer. The more effectively sellers apply the right questions and information, the more quickly and comfortably the buyer completes their decision process.

We know that customers have Internal Questions which they must ask and answer if they are to move forward in their purchase decision process. Since we know in advance what these questions are, we can prepare to provide decision makers with many of the answers. At the same time sellers should also prepare to ask questions so that they can accumulate the information needed to understand the customer's goals and how their solutions might best support those goals. *Cooperation Selling* provides sellers with proactive *Influence Questions* (IQ's) which are used to leverage influence and gain information from the customer. An example of how *Influence Questions* are leveraged with the buyer's *Internal Questions* in their first decision step *Acquire Information* looks like this:

| Seller Influence Questions | Customer Internal Questions |
|---|---|
| ✓ What do I know and how can I motivate the customer to consider making a decision? | ✓ Is making this decision important to me? |

| Seller Influence Questions | Customer Internal Questions |
| --- | --- |
| ✓ How can I help the customer to trust and work with me? | ✓ Which sources of information do I trust? |
| ✓ What could it cost the customer to not make a decision at this time? | ✓ What could it cost me to make or not make this decision? |

As this table illustrates, sellers can proactively prepare to guide customers in answering their Internal Questions by asking and answering the corresponding seller *Influence Questions* (IQ).

# Decision Leveraging: Influence Questions (IQ's) and Customer Internal Questions

The following are all of the Influence Questions (IQ's) covered in the *Cooperation Selling*™ methodology and their corresponding customer Internal Questions.

| Proactive Seller Influence Questions | Customer Internal Questions |
| --- | --- |
| ✓ What do I know and how can I motivate the customer to consider making a decision? | ✓ Is making this decision important to me? |
| ✓ How can I help the customer to trust and work with me? | ✓ Which sources of information do I trust? |
| ✓ What could it cost the customer to not make a decision at this time? | ✓ What could it cost me to make or not make this decision? |
| ✓ How can I help the customer get what they truly want and need? | ✓ How many possible decision choices are available and which one is best for me? |

| Proactive Seller Influence Questions | Customer Internal Questions |
|---|---|
| ✓ What are the customer's decision criteria and priorities? | ✓ What questions do I need answered before I can move forward with my decision? |
| ✓ How can I increase the customer's perception of differentiated value in me, my company and solution? | ✓ Do I still perceive enough value to move forward with my decision? |
| ✓ What can I do to best align our solutions with the customer's decision criteria? | ✓ Am I still comfortable with my decision criteria? |
| ✓ Why should the customer do business with us and not the competition? | ✓ Have I considered all of the decision options and chosen the one that is best for me? |
| ✓ How can we confirm agreements without confrontation? | ✓ Do I still perceive enough value in making the decision? |
| ✓ What can I do to ensure smooth implementation success? | ✓ Am I achieving the results I expected? |
| ✓ What can I do to help the customer achieve complete satisfaction? | ✓ Have my expectations changed? |
| ✓ Which are the best ways to improve customer relations while continuing to add to our bottom line? | ✓ Will I continue to do business with the provider company? |

As you can see, each of the *Influence Questions* (IQ's) proactively prepare the seller to either ask the customer questions or provide the customer with information that will aid them in answering their Internal Questions.

Chapter Five:

# Cooperation Selling Process

# Influence Steps Overview

*A simple yet powerful way to positively influence client decision making by improving the customer buying experience!*

In the *Cooperation Selling*™ process there are four *Influence Steps*. The real power of this selling methodology is that by combining buyer and seller intelligence, sellers more quickly synergize with their clients and remain customer-centrically connected throughout their entire buying decision process.

In subsequent chapters we will explore each of the four *Cooperation Selling-Influence Steps* in-depth. But for now let's start with an overview of how the *Cooperation Selling*™ methodology collaboratively combines the customer buying process with pro-active *Influence Steps* and decision leveraging.

We know that the customer buying decision process consists of four rational steps:

# Customer Buying Decision Process

Step One:     Acquire Information
Step Two:     Assess Options
Step Three:   Apply Decisions
Step Four:    Achieve Satisfaction

Each of the buying decision process steps was previously ex-plained. Now let's take a look at how the *Cooperation Selling-Influence Steps* merge with that process. Take note of how the Influence Questions (IQ) align with the Customer Internal Questions.

# Cooperation Selling Influence Steps

## Influence Step One: Uncover Opportunity

*Uncover Opportunity* is the first *Influence Step.* As sellers prepare to approach and engage prospects they should proactively prepare by considering the first three *Influence Questions* (IQ). This preparation is the most effective way for sellers to *Decision Leverage* their customer's buying decision process and Internal Questions.

Let's begin by considering the goals of the Seller in the *Uncover Opportunity* Influence Step:

- Uncover what might be the buyer's decision motivation – *What issues or problems might your customer be facing that would cause them to engage and consider a purchase decision?*
- Determine on which *Decision Tier* level your contact is located – *How should you position your message to best appeal to a person on this decision level?*

- Decide on an approach for contacting the customer – *Which approach will most likely lead to a successful contact?*
- Craft questions which will uncover the customer's understanding of their current condition vs. future condition – *What do you want the customer to really think about?*
- Answer customer questions and overcome any objections – *Which common questions or objections are you familiar with and how will you answer and overcome them?*
- Gain a Cooperation Commitment – *What actions might help the customer move forward after this conversation?*

Here are the *Influence Question* (IQ) and Customer Internal Question alignments for the seller's *Uncover Opportunity* and the customer's *Acquire Information* steps:

| Seller Influence Questions for Uncover Opportunity | Customer Internal Questions for Acquire Information |
|---|---|
| • What do I know and how can I motivate the customer to consider making a decision? | • Is making this decision important to me? |
| • How can I help the customer to trust and work with me? | • Which sources of information do I trust? |
| • What could it cost the customer to not make a decision at this time? | • What could it cost me to make or not make this decision? |

The seller's research, knowledge and experience should help to answer many of their IQ's prior to approaching the prospect. The rest of this step's *Influence Question* answers should be uncovered during the first engagement with the customer. Then the seller can leverage their prepared information along with any additional information that the customer might require in order to guide the customer through their *Acquire Information* internal questions.

# Influence Step Two: Refine Criteria

The seller's *Refine Criteria - Influence Step* begins while the customer is still answering *their Acquire Information* internal questions and continues into the customer's *Assess Options* buying decision step. Sellers should never assume that customers already know exactly what they want and need. In fact, they will be much better off to assume that the customer doesn't know for sure because they have not yet had the benefit of the knowledge and experience that the seller brings to their decision.

The *Refine Criteria - Influence Step* guides the customer to begin determining which goals, expectations and specific decision criteria should be used if they are going to move forward in their decision process. As the customer *Acquires Information* they consider whether a purchase at this time could be beneficial.

Using the *Refine Criteria* step, the seller:

• Determines if the customer has any additional decision motivations.
• Guides the customer in refining their list of decision priorities and criteria.

Consider the seller's goals during *Refine Criteria:*

- Continue to ask questions, listen carefully and keep two-way communications open.
- Uncover any additional decision influencers, their goals, level of influence, credibility and position in their decision process.
- Assist the customer in clarifying or refining their decision criteria.
- Ask discovery questions to insure that your customer's decision criteria list is complete, quantifiable and prioritized.
- Suggest useful, additional and possibly differentiating decision criteria.
- Confirm enough customer-perceived value to motivate your customer further into their decision process.

Let's review the *Influence Question* (IQ) and customer Internal Question alignment for the seller's *Refine Criteria* and the customer's *Assess Options* steps.

| Seller Influence Questions for Refine Criteria | Customer Internal Questions for Assess Options |
|---|---|
| • How can I help the customer to get what they truly want and need? <br><br> • What are the customer's decision criteria and priorities? <br><br> • How can I increase the customer's perception of differentiated value in me, my company and solution? | • How many possible decision choices are available and which one is best for me? <br><br> • What questions do I need answered before I can move forward with my decision? <br><br> • Do I still perceive enough value to proceed forward with my decision? |

The strategies and applications of the sellers Refine Criteria – Influence Step will guide the customer in creating and sorting their decision criteria and priorities. As the seller guides the customer closer to making their final purchase decision they will find the strategies and applications of their *Align Solution – Influence Step* extremely useful.

# Influence Step Three: Align Solution

At this point in the customer's decision process sellers should be well down the competitively differentiating road by performing their *Uncover Opportunity* and *Refine Criteria* decision influence steps. As sellers move to their *Align Solution - Influence Step* it becomes time to make sure that their final recommendations to the customer are going to completely satisfy them and move them toward their final purchase decision.

As the customer is transitioning from *Assess Options* to *Apply Decisions* they are attempting to determine whether they have enough information to make a safe decision and whether they still perceive enough current and future value in making the purchase. This means that the seller must begin to accomplish a new set of influence goals.

The Align Solution - Influence Step goals are:

- Know everything about the competition.
- Know everything about their own company and solution.
- Continue to gain competitive advantage.
- Deliver effective purchase decision recommendations *(by presentation if necessary)*.
- Continue to answer any customer provided questions.
- Acknowledge and overcome any customer objections.
- If required, negotiate to mutually beneficial conclusion.
- Confirm agreement and secure the customer partnership.

*Decision Leveraging* remains a critical asset in the *Align Solution* decision influence step. As the customer transitions into their *Apply Decisions* buying decision step they will begin coming to terms with the three internal questions that can be most challenging for them to answer over the course of their buying decision process.

How sellers handle themselves in the *Align Solution - Influence Step* will either confirm that they are a truly customer-centric, *Cooperation Selling*™ seller or they will be perceived by the customer to be just like everyone else!

Let's review the *Influence Questions* (IQ) and customer Internal Questions alignment for the seller's *Align Solution* and the customer's *Apply Decisions* steps.

| Seller Influence Questions for Align Solution | Customer Internal Questions for Apply Decisions |
|---|---|
| • What can I do to best align our solution with the customer's decision criteria?<br>• Why should the customer do business with us and not the competition?<br>• How can we confirm agreement without confrontation? | • Am I still comfortable with my decision criteria?<br>• Have I considered all of the available decision options and chosen the one that is best for me?<br>• Do I still perceive enough value to move forward in making the decision? |

The seller's *Align Solution* IQ's will guide the customer's purchase to a useful and equitable conclusion but the customer's buying decision process continues on to their final *Achieve Satisfaction* step. As the customer moves forward into their final decision step the seller guides this transition with their *Implement Agreement – Influence Step.*

## Influence Step Four: Implement Agreement

In the *Implement Agreement* Step the customers are asking themselves if they are satisfied with their purchase experience and decision. They also determine whether they are achieving the results they expected. Assuming that the seller met the customer's expectations and that they have performed the rest of their *Cooperation Selling*™ process effectively then the customer's answers to their questions should be 'Yes!'

In the *Implement Agreement* Influence Step sellers should continue using decision leveraging to ensure ultimate and complete customer satisfaction.

Let's review the seller's goals in the *Implement Agreement* Influence step:

- Understand and fulfill all of your customer's decision criteria and expectations.
- Proactively eliminate any delivery and implementation challenges.
- Aid the customer in quantifying expected deliverables.
- Improve the ongoing provider and customer relationship.
- Continue to provide "added value" for the customer over the lifecycle of the relationship.
- Nurture and grow the business partnership.
- Guide the customer to recognize and acknowledge "complete satisfaction."
- Gain additional business opportunities through customer introductions and referrals.

Just as it is in every other *Decision Influence Step*, the seller should continue to provide value to the customer and keep lines of communications open. If the seller intends to do additional business with the customer in the future, then they must do their very best to insure the greatest levels of continued customer satisfaction.

Let's review the *Influence Questions* (IQ) and customer Internal Question alignment for the seller's *Implement Agreement* and the customer's *Achieve Satisfaction* steps.

| Seller Influence Questions for Implement Agreement | Customer Internal Questions for Achieve Satisfaction |
|---|---|
| • What can I do to ensure smooth implementation success? | • Am I achieving the results I expected? |
| • What can I do to help the customer achieve complete satisfaction? | • Have my expectations changed? |
| • Which are the best ways to improve customer relations while continuing to add to our bottom line? | • Will I continue to do business with the provide company? |

# The Next Buying Decision Process

The *Cooperation Selling*™ methodology and process are depicted in a circle for a number of reasons. One of the more important reasons is that based on the customer's perception of seller behavior, the provider-customer relationship and levels of customer satisfaction the customer will determine if they will continue to do business with the seller.

If the seller has delivered a differentiated, customer-centric buying experience and if the customer is still satisfied, then the customer will choose to continue doing business with the seller. The more satisfied and comfortable the customer becomes, the more likely they will have additional trust in the seller. This can actually speed up the customer's decision process the next time they buy because as trust and credibility increases the customer's perceived risk in doing business with the seller decreases.

# Influence Question (IQ) and Customer Internal Question Associations

Let's review all of the Influence Steps, Influence Questions (IQ's), Buying Decision Steps and decision maker Internal Questions one last time to solidify the concept.

| DECISION INFLUENCE STEPS | BUYING DECISION STEPS |
|---|---|
| UNCOVER OPPORTUNITY | ACQUIRE INFORMATION |
| • What do I know and how can I motivate the customer to consider making a decision?<br>• How can I help the customer to trust and work with me?<br>• What could it cost the customer to not make a decision at this time? | • Is making this decision important to me?<br>• Which sources of information do I trust?<br>• What could it cost me to make or not make this decision? |

| DECISION INFLUENCE STEPS | BUYING DECISION STEPS |
|---|---|
| **REFINE CRITERIA** | **ASSESS OPTIONS** |
| • How can I help the customer to get what they truly want and need?<br>• What are the customer's decision criteria and priorities?<br><br>• How can I increase the customer's perception of differentiated value in me, my company and solution? | • How many possible decision choices are available and which one is best for me?<br>• What questions do I need answered before I can move forward with my decision?<br>• Do I still perceive enough value to proceed forward with my decision? |
| **ALIGN SOLUTION** | **APPLY DECISIONS** |
| • What can I do to best align our solution with the customer's decision criteria?<br>• Why should the customer do business with us and not the competition?<br><br>• How can we confirm agreement without confrontation? | • Am I still comfortable with my decision criteria?<br><br>• Have I considered all of the available decision options and chosen the one that is best for me?<br>• Do I still perceive enough value to move forward in making the decision? |
| **IMPLEMENT AGREEMENT** | **ACHIEVE SATISFACTION** |
| • What can I do to ensure smooth implementation success?<br>• What can I do to help the customer achieve complete satisfaction?<br>• Which are the best ways to improve customer relations while continuing to add to our bottom line? | • Am I achieving the results I expected?<br>• Have my expectations changed?<br><br>• Will I continue to do business with the provide company? |

# Chapter Six:

# Uncover Opportunity

# Decision Influence Step One: Uncover Opportunity

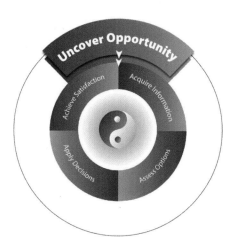

Uncover Opportunity is the first Influence Step. Let's begin by remembering the seller's goals:

- Determine the prospect's possible decision motivation – *What issues or problems might they be facing that would cause them to consider a purchase?*
- Determine the prospect's decision tier – *How should I position my message to be most appealing and motivating?*
- Decide on an approach for contacting the customer – *Which approach will most likely lead to a successful contact?*
- Craft questions which will uncover the customer's understanding of their current condition vs. future condition – *What do I want the customer to think about?*
- Answer customer questions and overcome any objections – *Why might they be or not be interested?*
- Gain a Cooperation Commitment – *How should we move forward after this conversation?*

It is also helpful to remember the *Influence Question* (IQ) and Customer Internal Question alignment for the Seller's *Uncover Opportunity* and the Customer's *Acquire Information* steps:

| Seller Influence Questions for Uncover Opportunity | Customer Internal Questions for Acquire Information |
|---|---|
| • What do I know and how can I motivate the customer to consider making a decision?<br>• How can I help the customer to trust and work with me?<br>• What could it cost the customer to not make a decision at this time? | • Is making this decision important to me?<br>• Which sources of information do I trust?<br>• What could it cost me to make or not make this decision? |

## Cooperation Selling™ begins with the right selling mindset!

It is important that sellers put their most differentiated foot forward and that begins with the right mindset. This mindset should be driven by the first of the three *Cooperation Selling – Core Values*:

1. Approach with "helping intentions"
2. Change the customer's experience
3. Demonstrate honesty and credibility

*(Note: For more information on the Cooperation Selling™ – Core Values refer to the 'Initiating Cooperation Selling' chapter.)*

Focusing on these values will increase seller's customer focus and ultimately provide a differentiation from other vendors.

*Remember: The way we think affects the way we feel, and the way we feel influences the way we behave!*

# Uncovering Buyer Cause Motivation

*Cooperation Selling Influence Questions* are used for seller proactive preparation and active engagement. Sellers should begin their preparation by considering the first of their *Uncover Opportunity - Influence Questions*:

---

**INFLUENCE QUESTION (IQ):** *What do I know and how can I motivate the customer to consider making a decision?*

---

What might motivate the customer to considering a purchase decision? If the seller's research uncovers some specific opportunity that they think will be an attractive motivation for the customer, then that usually becomes the center piece for the seller's approach conversation. This is called the "Motivating Cause" and it initiates the customer buying decision process. Often this motivating "Cause" involves some kind of change. This could be change in the industry or economy (external changes) or something uniquely specific to that company (internal changes). These are referred to as Change Forces.

The most common external Change Forces which have impact on every business are:

✓ Economic Shifts
✓ Government Regulations
✓ Competitive Shifts
✓ Their Customer's Needs
✓ Technology Introductions and Improvements

The most common internal Change Forces which can also impact every business are:

✓ Company Reorganizations or Restructuring
✓ Leadership Replacements or Introductions
✓ Corporate Direction and Vision Shifts
✓ New Product Development and Introduction
✓ Acquisitions & Mergers

# Primary Buyer Cause Motivations

There are three primary sources of buyer "Cause" motivations: Situation Repair, Situation Improvement and Situation Continuance.

## Situation Repair –Obvious Pain

With *Situation Repair* motivation, something is not functioning properly or producing at an effective level and must be repaired or replaced. The decision maker believes that if they do not take action then they may suffer painful or uncomfortable consequences. If the customer recognizes on their own that the situation is untenable then they may experience situation discomfort prior to the seller's approach.

An example of this might be if there is a competitive shift that causes the customer's competition to start acquiring more market share. The customer is aware that they are losing an unacceptable amount of business to the competition and are in what is called "obvious pain." If a seller is aware of this competitive shift and if they approach the customer with a possible solution for repairing their situation, then the customer may be very motivated to discuss a possible repair or resolution.

This is the customer situation that most sellers attempt identify and sell to. The reason is because traditional selling methodologies have instructed sellers to approach a prospect and ask questions to uncover obvious pain. Unfortunately, if the customer doesn't have obvious pain then they aren't usually motivated to purchase by the traditional approach. This is one of the best reasons why sellers should be aware of the second "Cause" motivation, *Situation Improvement*.

## Situation Improvement – Opportunity Pain

The second buyer "Cause" motivation is *Situation Improvement*. In the customer's opinion, nothing is broken but instead they realize that they are missing out on an improvement opportunity. This can be just as painful for the customer as Obvious Pain. Situation Improvement is a wonderful and frequently neglected prospecting opportunity. The reason it is commonly overlooked by sellers is simple; it generally requires more diagnostic questioning from the salesperson to uncover opportunity pain. Many salespeople don't pursue uncovering purchase motivation past the first brief conversation and in turn walk away from a huge number of potential sales.

Here's the good news! Just because the customer feels that everything is fine doesn't mean that they don't need or want help.

Once a customer understands that there is a possible unleveraged improvement opportunity, then they may become very motivated to engage in a conversation about a possible buying decision!

Common business improvement opportunities may include helping customers improve:

- ✓ Company Processes
- ✓ Departmental and Employee Interactions and Communications
- ✓ Employee Competency Development
- ✓ Leadership and Employee Organization
- ✓ Employee Productivity
- ✓ Market Share
- ✓ Customer Share

# Situation Continuance (Remaining Status Quo) – Decision Pain

The third buyer "Cause" motivation is Situation Continuance or remaining status quo. In this situation the customer is motivated to *not* make a purchasing decision at this time. This can be considered an "opposing motivator." In traditional selling the customer's choice to remain status quo is frequently considered to be the result of the seller not uncovering compelling "Obvious or Opportunity" pain. While this may be true in some cases, customers can actually be motivated away from making a decision. Issues driving this type of motivation include:

- They don't perceive the value in changing.
- Higher priorities are taking precedent.
- Other decision influencers are pressing the decision maker to focus on *their* priorities.

## People make purchase decisions in the time frame they choose!

One last thought about customers who choose to remain status quo rather than consider a purchase decision. If sellers recognize that this is actually a motivation and not a lack of motivation then they may also realize that they could still have a great opportunity to sell once the Situation Continuance motivational cause has been resolved, completed or eliminated.

Asking about what is motivating decision makers to remain status quo will help to determine an effective time line for following up with the prospect. With the future elimination of cause of the current motivation to remain status quo, the salesperson may stand a better chance of inspiring the customer toward a purchase decision at that time.

# Decision Making Tiers

*If beauty is in the eye of the beholder; then conversation value is in the mind of the customer!*

According to sellers a chronic challenge they face is getting decision makers and influencers to perceive enough value in partnering with them during their decision process. Traditional selling suggests that this situation occurs because either the salesperson is not talking to the right person or because their sales pitch is unappealing. I would suggest that neither is the case. Once the situation is analyzed the real challenge most frequently turns out to be that the seller was not speaking in the preferred terms or language based on the customer's *Decision Tier* responsibilities.

This leads us to the second of our *Uncover Opportunity - Influence Question*:

---

INFLUENCE QUESTION (IQ): *How can I help the customer to trust and work with me?*

---

*People don't mind talking about their work responsibilities and how they get measured performing them!*

One example of this can be recognized by any seller who has secured an appointment with a C-Level decision maker only to find that the person doesn't really want to talk to them. In many cases this situation is caused by the seller not conversing in in what the executive feels are relevant terms or conversation. For instance, if the seller is talking about how much money can be saved but the CEO is focused on improving market share then it is almost as if the seller is speaking an unimportant language.

It is critically important that sellers efficiently and effectively communicate with all levels of decision influencers about what is important to them. Let's consider the best way to make that happen.

## The Three Decision Tiers

Regardless of the size of an organization there are always three *Decision Making Tiers* in every organization. Although in some smaller organizations one person may be responsible for more than one tier of decision making, you can be sure that someone is always responsible for each level or tier. These three common decision tiers are:

- Leadership Tier
- Management Tier
- Producer Tier

Each of these decision tiers has their own unique work responsibilities associated with their job function, title or role in their company. The CEO of a company is normally responsible for things like the company vision, growth and profitability and would be considered a *Leadership Tier* decision maker. If a seller intends to engage the CEO in what they believe to be relevant conversation, then they stand the best chance of doing so by discussing the possible improvement of one or more of the CEO's responsibilities.

However, if a seller hopes to have a meaningful conversation with someone working in the Management Tier or the Producer Tier, those same topics will have far less relevance. And, if the conversation is deemed irrelevant by the decision maker or influencer then it is usually a short one.

Let's examine more closely the three *Decision Tiers.* We'll review each tier's basic responsibilities, what they are concerned about and what each should consider to be important and relevant conversation topics.

## Leadership Tier

The *Leadership Decision Tier* is associated with the C-Level or C-Suite. Job titles include Owner, CEO, CFO, CIO, COO, Executive Vice President and others who are in their own way responsible for growing the company top and bottom line.

Suggested conversation topics of interest for the *Leadership Tier* are usually connected to their job responsibilities and concerns. *Leadership Tier* common concerns are typically:

- ✓ Achieving Company Vision
- ✓ Profitability
- ✓ Revenue Growth
- ✓ Competitive Advantage
- ✓ Market Share
- ✓ Customer Share
- ✓ Employee Turnover
- ✓ Creating And Achieving Longer-Term Company Goals

# Management Tier

The *Management Decision Tier* is associated with the mid-level management positions in most companies. These managers are normally responsible for the core processes of the company.

Core processes are activities or tasks, which if not properly or consistently performed, will cause the company to fail in its primary mission. These core processes can fall into many business areas which may include things like design, production, sales & marketing and the supporting departments such as IT, HR, etc.

Conversation topics of interest for the Management Tier are also usually connected to their job responsibilities and concerns. *Management Tier* concerns are typically:

- ✓ Supporting And Achieving Leadership's Created Goals
- ✓ Employee Development
- ✓ Achieving Determined Business Objectives
- ✓ Team Building
- ✓ Generating and Increasing Team Productivity

✓ Customer Retention
✓ Driving, Monitoring and Improving Processes

## Producer Tier

The *Producer Decision Tier* is associated with the front-line employees who are responsible for producing the work of their role, team and department. These employees are responsible for following rules, directives and procedures. *Producer Tier* concerns are things like:

✓ Fulfilling Their Daily Job Requirements
✓ Following Standard Operating Procedures
✓ Adhering to Management and Leadership Directives
✓ Not Making Mistakes
✓ Achieving Shorter-Term Goals
✓ Maintaining Assigned Spending Budgets

If sellers are going to be most effective then they should understand how decision makers and influencers make decisions and they should know how to effectively communicate with any one of them at any level of a company, enterprise or organization.

# Approaching the Prospect

It's been said that you never get a second chance to make a first impression. Any experienced seller already understands the negative impact of not making an effective first contact. Hopefully a better understanding of what to look for when uncovering buyer "Cause" motivation will inspire sellers to be more on target when making their initial prospecting approach. However, you should probably keep this in mind:

## *Don't waste time looking for a magical motivator!*

I've witnessed sellers staring at their computer screens for hours in hopes of finding the golden topic to begin their approach. If at all possible it is important to determine what specific "motivational cause" might generate the most initial interest for the prospect. But if the seller doesn't have a specifically linked *Situation Repair* or *Situation Improvement* topic to broach with the prospect then a high probability Change Force may offer enough initial conversation interest for the customer. Sellers need to quickly determine what might be the best reasons for making the contact and then just do it!

The most common resources used for researching an effective buyer "Cause" motivation include:

- ✓ Social Networking (*LinkedIn, Facebook, Twitter, etc.*)
- ✓ The Customer's Website
- ✓ Customer Published Press Releases
- ✓ Required Customer Business and Financial Filings (*10k, 8k, Annual Reports, etc.*)
- ✓ Paid Research Sources (*One Source, Hoovers, Inside View, etc.*)
- ✓ Internally Provided Customer Relationship Management (CRM) Software

## Social Media Prospecting

Because of the popularity of social media venues there is a lot of prospect information available. Social media also provides a more easily accepted introduction opportunity than other traditional approaches. Just don't let yourself get caught in the trap of thinking that social media is all that is needed for business to business selling.

## *I've never heard of a "One Tweet" close!*

The idea of selling via social media and completely eliminating traditional prospecting methods is no doubt alluring and yet completely unachievable in most B2B (business to business) selling industries. But social media does provide very attractive channels for broadening a seller's holistic prospecting plan, generating more warm leads and becoming known, liked and even trusted prior to their initial selling contact with a prospect.

Sellers should realize that the true social media opportunity is to:

✓ Identify High Potential Prospects
✓ Generate SME (Subject Matter Expert) Creditability
✓ Gather Information to Support Prospect Decision Motivation

## Identifying High Potential Prospects

As part of a well-rounded and balanced prospecting plan social networking provides sellers contact opportunities that may not be otherwise as easily discovered or accessible. By identifying key words, key hash tags and high potential groups of interest, the opportunity to connect with warm leads is certainly worth investing time with social media. Just remember that the true opportunity provided by social media is to identify prospects with some level of interest prior to contact or engagement.

## *Social Media prospecting is about learning; not selling!*

Social media provides a wonderful platform for learning about and engaging a target audience with meaningful information and conversation. Just as customers are doing more research prior to making purchase decisions, it only makes sense that sellers should learn helpful and prospect guiding information prior to their initial engagement.

Lead generation is really about identifying new business opportunities as well as opening new doors in some target accounts. So by using similar "key words" that your company might use for marketing, sellers can identify groups, articles, hash tag chats and blogs which offer listening and learning opportunities. Listening and learning helps to leverage social intelligence into warm lead contact opportunities. Just remember that social media is an "opening tool" not a closing tool.

## Generate SME (Subject Matter Expert) Credibility

Becoming a trusted advisor has been a long time goal for many sellers. Sellers know that working themselves into a position of trust and confidence with their clients is important if they are going to become their client's provider of choice.

## *It is always better to add value to a conversation than it is to control it!*

After reading thousands of posted articles, blogs and hash tag chat comments it appears to me that a lot of people seem to think that they can prove that they are a subject matter expert by disagreeing with the posted opinions and ideas of others.

Attempting to convert and control the conversation in an effort to prove that you are right and others are wrong creates opposing opinions more frequently than supporting ones.

Instead, consider taking the high road and adding value to the conversation when possible and simply avoid adding negative or disagreeable comments. You will earn more new contacts with support and kindness than you will with disagreement and argument.

It is recommended that sellers use their experience, knowledge and expertise to augment and add value to conversations by sharing information and ideas that others have not posted. If this is done regularly within the seller's choice forums, then over time they will establish themselves as a credible and positive experts and influencers with those who they support. Sellers will certainly find the reception warmer when they reach out to high potential prospects who already consider them to be a positive influence and SME. If sellers want to be popular with social media networks and receive better responses to their prospect engagements, then they should become the person who offers support and answers. Share information freely and through your positive and supporting behavior encourage others to do the same.

## Gather Information To Support Prospect Decision Motivation

Sellers can improve the quality of their future prospect engagements by monitoring target prospects and managing their online presence. Reviewing target company blogs and other internet postings, following target prospects and/or their company while participating in social media prospecting aids sellers in gathering real time information about the prospect's needs and opinions. Sellers don't need to know everything about a prospect before making initial contact, but any information they do collect can be used to initially engage the person or company in what is likely to be more meaningful initial conversation. By paying attention to and listening to what is being said by and about the prospect then sellers can prepare a high pay-off approach for their initial engagement. Knowing who to call, when to call and why the prospect might be motivated to talk makes sellers far more effective with warm lead opportunities.

## *Social media prospecting creates tomorrow's warm leads!*

Social media prospecting should be considered a portion of a sellers overall prospecting plan. It requires patience and a commitment to the core value of 'Approach with helping intentions.' As long as sellers understand that social media is best used for prospecting and not closing then their efforts go a long way in setting up sales for tomorrow and they can become very powerful warm lead generators.

Popular prospecting research avenues can generate a considerable amount of information. However, there are really only three, very basic yet absolutely important things that the salesperson must determine before making initial contact.

The three things that sellers should know when making an approach:

1. Who is the Crucial Decision Maker?
2. What is the best initial Buyer Cause Motivation?
3. What is the best approach method to reach the Crucial Decision Maker?

## IMPORTANT: Who is the Crucial Decision Maker?

The *Crucial Decision Maker* is predominately a *Leadership Tier* decision maker who has the most to gain or lose by making or not making the intended purchase decision. This is the person in any organization who possesses enough influence and credibility to either make the buying decision themselves or engage a decision influence group for making the decision. (*We will review more about the Crucial Decision Maker in the Selling to Decision Influence Groups chapter.*)

## IMPORTANT: What is the best initial Buyer "Cause" Motivation?

This is the topic that sellers use to generate enough initial interest to motivate the prospect into an extended first conversation or to schedule a first meeting. (*Keep in mind that the initial "Cause" motivation should be something that the seller believes is of reasonable importance to the customer and is also something that they can help repair or improve.*)

## IMPORTANT: What is the best Method of Approach?

The seller should determine which approach method they will use to engage the customer. This is based on their knowledge of the identified decision maker or their experiences with similar decision makers and companies.

# Customer Approach Methods

Despite the myriad of communication methods that we can use to contact a Crucial Decision Maker, there are still only three ways for sellers to make an initial prospecting approach:

1. Approach in Person
2. Approach in Writing
3. Approach with a Telephone Call

Every seller seems to have their "preferred" method of approach and they always seem to lean very heavily on their preference. Sellers will admit, however, that their preferred approach will not connect them with every customer that they hope to engage.

I would suggest that if you are comfortable with the approach method you are currently using and if you are achieving reasonable selling success, then keep using it! Don't stop doing what is working for you. Yet isn't it possible that even your favorite approach method might be improved? This is just one of the reasons why so many great sellers track their selling efforts to determine what really works and what doesn't.

*I must record and quantify my selling behaviors and activities so I can continually measure my abilities, improvement areas and successes.*

By tracking their approach methods and outcomes a seller can more easily and effectively answer the following questions:

- Whicoh approach method produces the best results?
- Which buyer "Cause" motivation captures the most initial customoer interest?
- Which approach methods have not been used consistently?

The answers to these questions can be revealing. So here is the recommendation:

*STRATEGY: Continue to improve on the approach method you prefer but also start working on and improving the other two methods because they will be needed.*

We are now going to examine the three methods for approaching a prospect. As you choose the method of approach you intend to use it is important that you keep the third *Uncover Opportunity* – Influence Question in mind.

---

INFLUENCE QUESTION (IQ): *What could it cost the customer to <u>not</u> make a decision at this time?*

---

Asking and answering this (IQ) *Influence Question* will help you to identify the buyer "Cause" motivations that will yield the best results. You will see how this plays out in the examples that follow.

## The Telephone Call Approach – The 3 C's

Flatter organizations, increased decision maker work responsibilities and layers of contact screeners have made the initial contact with executives more difficult than ever. Even though using the telephone to make an initial approach is not the predominately preferred method used by sellers today, large numbers are still very successful using it. According to those successful sellers the most effective telephone approach procedures are those that are well planned and consistently executed. This is exactly why I suggest using the 3 C's Telephone Approach. The 3 C's in this approach represent the three components of the procedure which are *Courtesy, Cause and Commitment.*

STRATEGY: Courtesy, Cause and Commitment

*Courtesy:* Sellers should be mindful that the people they contact have many responsibilities and are frequently under a time crunch to handle their work priorities. Given that, they should respect the customer's time when making contact. If sellers find that the person doesn't have time for a conversation at the moment of contact, then scheduling another time for the call is the right thing to do.

Some examples of how to exhibit courtesy toward the customer and their time are:

*"I know you're very busy so I appreciate you accepting my call." Or, "I know you probably have a lot going on today so I'll be brief."*

Simply showing professional courtesy for their time and other priorities can go a long way in immediately differentiating sellers from others who have called.

*Cause:* Presenting a possible "Cause" statement as part of your introduction is the best way to gather a customer's attention and motivate them into a longer discussion or future appointment. This is the first real opportunity that the seller has to "influence" the customer's decision process. With the presentation of an effective "Cause" statement comes the opportunity to explore the customer's current condition and find ways to improve their future situation. The seller can use one specific motivating cause or a combination of possible Change Force influences to construct their "Cause" motivation statement. Just remember to tailor the "*Cause*" statement to the Decision Tier you are speaking to.

*"We've helped companies like Kerner Supply, One Stop and Quality Supply improve both their productivity and profitability. I believe that we can do the same for you!"*

*Commitment:* The purpose of a seller's commitment question is to gain the prospect's agreement to continue the conversation. Whether the specific objective is to continue the conversation at that moment or schedule some future meeting, sellers need the agreement of the customer to do so. Examples of a "Commitment" questions are:

*"May we get together sometime next week to discuss how Global Enterprises can help achieve your goals?"*

Or,

*"Do you have a few minutes to explore how Global Enterprises helps customers to achieve their goals?"*

If the customer tells you it is not a good time to continue the conversation, don't fall into the traditional selling method trap of trying to spew information at them in some futile attempt to create value. If you remember the reasons for showing Courtesy in the first place, then maybe it truly isn't the best time for the customer to share their attention with you. Your *helping intentions* might be better served if you simply appear understanding and ask the next obvious question:

*"What would be the best time for us to speak?"* Or, *"I understand completely, when would be a better time for us to have a brief conversation?"*

You are more likely to acquire the customer's full attention by scheduling a time of their choosing. Don't attempt to convince them that their current focus is not as important as what you want to talk about. Also by making an appointment and keeping it, you demonstrate the *Cooperation Selling* - Core Value *"Demonstrate Honesty and Credibility."*

Once the *Commitment* to continue the conversation or meet with the seller has been obtained then the real influence opportunity begins. Sellers should view the customer's commitment to continue their conversation as a sign of initial decision interest. But sellers should also keep in mind that the customer isn't communicating that they are ready to buy. Instead they are conveying that they are willing to engage, communicate and listen. The prospect is presenting the seller with a commitment of time to be used by the seller to help them decide whether they have enough motivation to move forward in their decision process.

By combining three of the *Courtesy, Cause and Commitment* component examples, then the actual telephone approach might go something like this:

## Approach Opening:
*Hello. I'm Sales Superstar with Global Enterprises.*

| Courtesy | *I know you probably have a lot going on today so I'll be brief.* |
| --- | --- |
| Cause | *We've helped companies like Kerner Supply, One Stop and Quality Supply improve both their productivity and profitability. I believe that we can do the same for you!* |
| Commitment | *May we get together sometime next week to discuss how Global Enterprises might help achieve your goals?* |

Once the seller has obtained the customer's initial commitment to continue then it is time to begin helping the customer to flesh out decision motivating answers to their *Acquire Information* internal questions.

# The In-Person Approach

Once again, when preparing to approach a prospect in person the first thing you should think about is, which decision tier will you be contacting? Each decision tier has their own motivating causes based on their work assignment and responsibilities. Recognize the different motivational causes and blend those into your initial conversation.

Here is an example of the "In Person" approach to a *Leadership Tier* decision maker.

*Good morning! I'm David Spears with Mutual Benefit Incorporated. We help companies improve profitability, customer retention and overall employee satisfaction. I'd like you speak with you to determine whether we might help you in some of the same ways that we have so many other companies. Do you have time for a brief meeting right now?*

As you consider this example I would like to bring to light one portion of the approach that may raise concern for some traditional selling thinkers. I'm referring to the commitment question, "Do you have time for a brief meeting right now?"

Sellers should realize that if they are fortunate enough to get face to face with the *Crucial Decision Maker*, the odds of them being completely available at that specific moment for a meeting or discussion are not always likely. In fact, it is more likely that the person will be already engaged with work issues and even if they agreed to a conversation their attention may be otherwise engaged. Just like in the Telephone Approach, sellers should always respect their customer's time. This means that when we make an In Person approach we should consider asking the decision maker "Is now a good time?" Or at the very least we should show courtesy by suggesting that the initial meeting will be brief. So be courteous of the customer's time and if they are too busy at the moment for a meeting or discussion then just ask the next logical and appropriate question:

*I completely understand. What might be a better time for us to have a brief meeting?*

    I would suggest that if it isn't a good time for the customer and they are willing to schedule another meeting time with you that they are far more likely to be focused on the conversation and the value you bring at that time. Isn't that one of the things we hope to accomplish in an initial meeting or engagement?

*It's always better to have a great first meeting in the future than a mediocre meeting now!*

    If the customer is preoccupied with other issues when you meet them then, out of simple courtesy, ask to schedule your initial meeting for a future time of their choosing and you will normally find that they are much more receptive and attentive at that time.

## The Written Approach

    "Written" doesn't necessarily mean this approach has to be delivered in the form of a traditional letter. According to some of the best sellers, they use multiple communication channels and even forum style mediums such as Linked-in, Facebook, or other business and social media networks.

Some of these networks provide an enhanced contact opportunity allowing sellers to bypass screeners and make direct contact with the *Crucial Decision Maker*. One example of this is the Linked-In InMail. InMail has a much higher received and read rate than traditional e-mail and can be sent without a formal introduction and connection. (Note that InMail and similar services may only be included as part of an upgraded service.)

There are proven best practice components sellers should consider if they want their written approach to be as powerful as possible. These components include:

- ✓ Introduction and Possible Uniqueness
- ✓ Interest Statement
- ✓ Credibility Statement
- ✓ Possible Cause Motivation
- ✓ Suggested Intention
- ✓ Action Commitment

Some communication methods may limit the length of a message. By understanding what each of these components can do, it may help sellers to choose the best ones for their chosen delivery mechanism and written communication size.

## STRATEGY: Consider using compelling components in your written approach

Component #1 - *Introduction and Possible Uniqueness:* This lets the prospects know who you are; who or what you represent and if possible, what makes you uniquely qualified or inspired to contact them. An example of this could be:

*"I represent Global Enterprises Inc. the industry leader in demographic specific marketing."*

**Component #2 - *Interest Statement:*** An Interest Statement suggests to the customer that you intend to discuss something that is probably important to them at their decision tier. Here is an Interest Statement tailored to the Leadership Tier:

*"Increasing your base of new motivated customers while maintaining acceptable profit margins has never been more important or difficult."*

**Component #3 - *Credibility Statement:*** This tells the prospect that you have earned the trust of businesses similar to theirs. An example of a Credibility Statement might look like this:

*"We've helped companies like Westwind Manufacturing and Big-Time Supply improve their market positions while increasing profits more than 11% in less than six months!"*

*(Please note that sellers should never state or quote statistics or facts which they cannot readily prove. In doing so, they may ruin any credibility, trust or relationship opportunities which they hoped to create.)*

**Component #4 - *Possible Cause Motivation:*** Suggesting buyer "Cause" motivation is important if the seller hopes to create enough motivation to obtain an initial prospect engagement. This is crucial and can involve several Change Forces or something specific to that customer. Here is an example:

*"We can help your sellers gain more direct access to actual decision makers to ensure that your marketing strategies are ultimately more powerful, successful and profitable."*

**Component #5 - *Suggested Intention:*** This statement expresses what the seller would like to do or what they would like to request from the customer. This can be as simple as:

*"I would like to schedule a brief meeting with you."*

Component #6 - *Action Commitment:* It is important that the seller provide a suggested Action Commitment statement (or request) so that the prospect can begin to determine whether or not the seller is trustworthy. By offering an Action Commitment and then following through on that proposed commitment the seller begins to show that they can be trusted. An example might be:

*"I will call you on Tuesday the 21st at 8:15 am in order to schedule our meeting."*

This commitment statement should be followed with the salesperson's contact information if they think that the prospect may already possess enough motivation to respond as a result of this written approach contact.

If we put all of the suggested written approach component examples together in letter format, then here's what the *Written Approach* might look like:

Mr. Decision Maker
CEO – Future Electronics
1000 Sonic Speed Dr.
Starlight, VA 55555

Dear Crucial Decision Maker,

I represent Global Enterprises Inc. the industry leader in demographic specific marketing.

Increasing your base of new motivated customers while maintaining acceptable profit margins has never been more important or difficult.

We've helped companies like Westwind Manufacturing and Big-Time Supply improve their market positions while increasing profits more than 11% in less than six months! (Proof sources available on request.)

We can help your sellers gain more direct access to actual decision makers to ensure that your marketing strategies are ultimately more powerful, successful and profitable.

I would like to schedule a brief meeting with you to share in more detail how Global Enterprises helps our customer partners become more successful in less time. I will call you on next Tuesday the 21st at 8:15 am in order to schedule our meeting. Should you desire to contact me sooner, please feel free to call me directly at 555.555.1234 or e-mail me at s.superstar@globalenterprises.com

Thank you in advance for your interest in our meeting,

Sales Superstar
Senior Corporate Account Representative
Global Enterprises, Inc.

(This is an education example only and does not represent actual company names and/or interests.)

# Navigating Premature Price Questions

At times during an initial contact with a customer, this question arises: "Can you give me a ballpark price?" or "Give me an idea of how much we're talking about?" When this comes up you should recognize that what the customer is really attempting to determine is the answer to their first or third Acquire *Information* internal questions, "*Is making this decision important to me?*" and/or "*What could it cost me to make or not make this decision?*"

When the *ballpark* or similar question is asked so early then it probably means that they have a small degree of motivation (*probably suggested by the Cause statement*) but not enough motivation to move forward in their decision process. So it is doubtful that the prospect is trying to decide if they want to buy. Instead I would suggest that they are probably thinking "Do I want to continue talking to the seller?"

This is why this question occurs so frequently when sellers are making first contact and attempting to secure an appointment. The customer asks the question because they are attempting to compare their current situation against the cost of continuing the conversation or scheduling the meeting with the seller. The "ballpark" question is not a bad thing as long as sellers don't misinterpret it. The strategy recommended by the best sellers is a possible three stage approach.

## STRATEGY: Refocus the customer on the conversation instead of the price!

*(Stage 1 and/or 2 may be enough to refocus the prospect and conversation.)*

If the customer asks for a ballpark price, then suggest:

**STAGE 1:** *I can do better than that! I can give you an exact price but we'll need to exchange a little more information before I'm comfortable doing that. Would that be OK?*

If the customer says yes, then continue the conversation or ask for the meeting. If the customer asks a second time, then consider using the next step.

**STAGE 2:** *Mr. Customer, I'm sure you understand that we wouldn't be the (local, industry or marketplace) leader if we weren't price competitive. But in order for me to determine which solution is best for you and then provide you with specific pricing I need to ask a few more questions. Would that be ok?*

If the customer agrees then the seller should continue forward with their questions and conversation. But if the customer asks a third time about price then the seller needs to make a choice.

Another reason the customer is asking so soon about pricing might be that they are attempting to determine whether the proposed purchase is within their budget. If that seems to be the case, the seller's next step would be to suggest a "range" of pricing based on their current understanding of what the customer might need.

If the seller believes that the customer does not yet perceive enough value in what they have to offer at this time, then their next step would be to suggest the postponement of the conversation until a future meeting. There could be other customer issues or priorities that are preventing the customer from focusing on the conversation with the seller. If this is what the seller believes the situation to be then they might say something like:

STAGE 3: *"It appears that this may not be the best time for you to think about this. I know that you have a lot going on. Would you prefer to reschedule our meeting for a future time?"*

If the customer chooses to continue, then sellers should continue with their planned questions and conversation. If the customer chooses to reschedule then it would be best to do so.

# Cooperation Commitments

*Cooperation Commitments are stated intentions by both the provider and customer to perform actions that should help the customer to move forward in their decision process.*

Over the years I've fielded thousands of seller questions from dozens of industries. There are two selling questions which get most frequently asked:

1. When should I disengage from a prospect?
2. What is the best way to forge the right selling relationship with my customers?

Even though these two questions might appear to be on opposite ends of the selling spectrum; both can be answered with one strategy. The strategy is called *Cooperation Commitments*.

## SELLING BENEFIT: Selling Disengagement

The first *Cooperation Selling* core value is *"Approach with helping intentions."* This includes helping the customer to make a decision. The goal of *Cooperation Selling*™ is to harmonize the intentions and actions of the provider and customer. In fact, the expected outcome of selling this way is that selling and buying become synchronized into a partnership of decision effort. But if for their own reasons the customer chooses to stop moving forward in their decision process and the seller cannot currently influence them enough become more motivated then it is time for the seller to disengage.

Selling disengagement is to professionally withdraw from active selling when, despite the seller's best efforts to motivate them, the customer has chosen to no longer move forward.

Considering disengagement should occur after the seller has begun to question whether there is anything else they might do to motivate the decision maker forward in their decision process. Disengagement doesn't mean that the seller won't continue to communicate with the customer after disengagement. Some customer business situations may change and if so then the seller will want to reengage at that time.

## SELLING BENEFIT: Relationship Development

Knowing how to forge the right selling relationship is important to any career selling professional. And yet this seemingly lofty goal continues to elude many sellers. The challenge is most likely a misunderstanding of customer expectation.

Many salespeople have been taught that customers want and expect service. The appropriate interpretation of "service" in this context is that customers want and expect reasonable support when making their decision and maintaining satisfaction after their purchase. But many sellers think that wanting and expecting service means that the onus is on the seller to do all of the work "for" the customer in their decision process. With this mindset, sellers begin to behave as if they must "earn" the customer's business by working hard and do everything for them. Unfortunately, this mindset can actually hinder relationship development.

## It takes <u>two</u> people working together to forge a relationship!

It takes at least *two* people working together to forge a relationship! If the seller is doing all of the work for the customer because they believe that will improve the customer's willingness to buy, then the customer is not really investing energy in their own decision. Without both parties working together toward the customer's best decision it becomes almost impossible to forge any meaningful relationship.

## Participation creates buy-in, ownership and adaptability!

The more the customer participates in their own decision process the more probable they will:

- Buy into needed change and transitions.
- Accept ownership for the changes and decisions which must be made for improvement.
- Adapt more quickly to new mindsets, attitudes and procedures.

Partnering relationships are created because two or more people choose to work together toward a common goal. When forging a professional selling and buying relationship with the customer or when effectively determining when the seller should disengage from the customer the best strategy is to ask for and obtain *Cooperation Commitments*.

## STRATEGY: Ask for and obtain Cooperation Commitments

*Cooperation Commitments* are stated intentions by both the seller and customer to perform some action that should help the customer to move forward in the decision process. As this occurs then both parties are working to improve the odds that the customer will make their best decision. At the same time the seller and customer become partners in the customer's decision process.

If the customer is unwilling to commit to performing tasks that will help them to move forward in their decision process, then what is probably lacking is enough motivating Cause to do so. This can result for several reasons:

- The customer feels that the challenges of making the decision have become greater than the original motivations which started their decision.
- The seller didn't uncover enough motivation to drive the whole decision process.
- Some outside influence has caused the decision maker to rethink the timing or value of their purchase decision.

So *Cooperation Commitments* are asked for and obtained by sellers to:

- ✓ Drive better purchase decision motivation.
- ✓ Create a sense of control and decision commitment for the customer.
- ✓ Create and enhance the partnering relationship opportunity between the seller and the customer.

Some examples of *Cooperation Commitments* which sellers might ask for and obtain from customers are:

- Providing information critical to formulating or validating decision criteria, purchase recommendations or the customer's final decision.
- Inviting other important or relevant influencers into the decision process.
- Reviewing information provided by the seller which is intended to educate the customer.
- Questioning other decision influencers for input and information.
- Coordinating decision influencers in an effort to move the decision process forward.

These agreed upon tasks should be performed by the customer prior to speaking to the seller again and should always help to move the customer forward in the decision process.

## Three *Cooperation Commitment components:*

COMPONENT 1: The seller's commitment to perform one or more tasks that should help the customer to move forward in their decision process

COMPONENT 2: The requested or suggested task(s) for the customer to complete before the next conversation or meeting and should also help the customer to move forward in their decision process

COMPONENT 3: The commitment confirmation question.

Example of a Cooperation Commitment:

*"Before we speak again, I'm going to look up the specifications to confirm that what we are considering for you is the best possible solution. And I would ask that you speak with your employees and determine whether there are any other decision criteria we should be considering. Does that sound acceptable?"*

## Ask for a Cooperation Commitment every time you talk to a customer!

Always ask for a *Cooperation Commitment* at the end of every meeting or conversation with a customer. By doing so the salesperson creates a gauge for repeatedly determining and confirming the customer's level of decision motivation.

# The Message of Intent (MOI)

A Message of Intent is one of the best ways to encourage the customer's completion of *Cooperation Commitments* and to maintain a record of any other agreements either offered or obtained during customer engagement. This also ensures that the seller will make fewer mistakes and eliminate misunderstandings between the two parties.

It is recommended that soon after the seller has completed their conversation or meeting they should send a brief e-mail reiterating the conversation, any conclusions derived and any commitments offered and obtained. The following are two examples of the *Message of Intent*.

## Example One:

Mr. Customer,

Thank you for your time and hospitality during our meeting. As I'm sure we can both agree, it was time well invested. Per our discussion, I'll gather the information you requested and prepare to meet with your staff next Wednesday morning. I appreciate your leadership on this initiative and taking the time to arrange for my meeting with your staff. I promise that we'll achieve valuable results and I'll be sensitive to keeping the meeting as short as possible.

Please feel free to contact me if anything changes or if you develop any questions.

Thank you for your commitment to excellence,

Sales Superstar
(Signature Block)

## Example Two:

Mr. Customer,

I appreciate you meeting with me and openly sharing your concerns about your current provider relationships. As promised, I will secure and bring the overview information you asked for to our next meeting and I look forward to finding out what your interviews with your employees revealed. I believe that you are correct in that by speaking to each of them you should be able to gain a better understanding of what they like and don't like about your current providers. I believe that your leadership in this initiative will yield important and useful results.

Please contact me prior to our scheduled meeting if anything changes or if you develop any additional questions.

Thank you for your commitment to excellence,

Sales Superstar
(Signature Block)

# Information, Applications and Outcomes

As with most educational experiences this book provides the reader with information which they may not have previously possessed. New information is always good for stimulating new ideas and can sometimes help to reshape our perceptions and behavior. But in order for the information to have the best chance of being effectively used, the transition from information to application must occur.

Please consider taking the time to answer the provided questions in order to begin your own information to application transition. These transitions will help to guarantee the fastest and most useful applications and outcomes in your selling career.

*What Information was provided in this chapter that you felt was important and possible useful to you?*

*How might you apply these important points of information?*

*What outcomes do you hope or expect to produce as a result of your application implementations?*

# Chapter Seven:

# Refine Criteria

# Decision Influence Step Two: Refine Criteria

Before we take a closer look at the second decision influence step let's review the goals that create the most effective seller mindset. The goals for the Refine Criteria influence step are:

- Continue to ask questions, listen carefully and keep two-way communications open.
- Uncover any additional decision influencers, their goals, level of influence, credibility and position in their decision process.
- Assist the customer in clarifying or refining their decision criteria.
- Ask "DISCcovery" questions to insure that the customer's decision criteria list is complete, quantifiable and prioritized.
- Suggest useful, additional and possibly differentiating decision criteria.
- Confirm enough customer-perceived value to motivate the customer further into their decision process.

Consider again the *Influence Question* (IQ) and customer Internal Question alignment for the seller's *Refine Criteria* and the customer's *Assess Options* steps.

| Seller Influence Questions for Refine Criteria | Customer Internal Questions for Assess Options |
|---|---|
| • How can I help the customer to get what they truly want and need?<br>• What are the customer's decision criteria and priorities?<br>• How can I increase the customer's perception of differentiated value in me, my company and solution? | • How many possible decision choices are available and which one is best for me?<br>• What questions do I need answered before I can move forward with my decision?<br>• Do I still perceive enough value to proceed forward with my decision? |

When customers begin their first buying decision step, *Acquire Information*, they recognize enough initial motivation to engage with the seller in a longer conversation or first meeting. But, this does not mean that they have enough information or motivation to complete their decision process and they are rarely prepared to complete their purchase! If the customer is to continue forward in their decision process they have additional internal questions which will need to be answered.

The seller should use the strategies in their *Refine Criteria* step to enhance the customer's motivation to complete their *Acquire Information* buying decision step and then guide them forward to begin answering their *Assess Options* buying decision step Internal Questions.

## Early sales pitches encourage customer resistance!

Entrenched selling wisdom suggests that sellers should acquire a customer's attention and then "pitch" early in the seller-buyer engagement. Many sellers have been taught that early pitching should enhance decision maker perceptions of purchase value. In reality, interviewed customers suggest that the opposite is true.

The early sales pitch is more likely going to cause unwanted resistance from the customer rather than create any additional perception of value. The reason is simple: People prefer to walk a path of self-discovery in their decision making rather than being pitched or pushed down their decision path. This is because people are more likely to believe in and act on with enthusiasm what they think themselves rather than what they are told by someone else.

*People are more likely to accept and act on what they deduce for themselves... not what they are told!*

As customers begin their *Assess Options* decision step, sellers should not assume that they already know exactly what they want or need. Customers don't usually possess the seller's depth of knowledge about available products and services. It is also likely that the customer will need assistance doing a deep and valid assessment of their current situation and their future goals in order to determine what they might really need. Sellers should also keep in mind that the customer may have been influenced by a competitor and that valuable information or criteria may have been overlooked!

---

INFLUENCE QUESTION (IQ): *How can I help the customer get what they truly want and need?*

---

To be most effective in assisting customers when answering their *Assess Options* internal questions, sellers should again remember their *Cooperation Selling – Core Values*. The four critical core values to exhibit in the *Refine Criteria* decision influence step are:

- ✓ Ask and Listen.
- ✓ Be Open Minded.
- ✓ Create an Environment of Support.
- ✓ Know Everything About Your Solution.

*(Note: For more information on the Cooperation Selling™ – Core Values refer to the 'Initiating Cooperation Selling' chapter.)*

Customers are more open to seller influence once they understand that the seller actually does care about them, their situation and their needs. One of the complaints that customers express about their interactions with sellers is that the salesperson didn't or wouldn't listen. This non-listening behavior is what can begin to convince customers that all sellers are the same and that they primarily care about themselves. Making a noticeable effort to *Ask and Listen* will differentiate the seller as one who does indeed care about the customer, their needs and their business.

## STRATEGY: Use the "Please Repeat" approach to more effectively "Ask and Listen."

When exhibiting the core value behavior of *Ask and Listen,* one strategy that sellers may find useful is the "Please Repeat" approach. As you're asking questions and listening to the answers always make sure that you hear and understand everything that the customer communicates. This strategy will prove to the customer that you are listening. This technique is extremely useful when discerning and positively influencing the customer's decision criteria and priorities. Here's how the strategy works:

Please Repeat Technique:

*Listen to the customer's answers to your questions and if they mention something you believe is important to them then say, "That sounded important. Would you please repeat that?"*

**STRATEGY:** Use the "Statement of Intention" technique to display open mindedness.

The best way to internalize and follow the core value *Be Open Minded* is to remain unconvinced that what you have to offer is what the customer actually needs until you have uncovered all of the customer's decision criteria. Instead of pitching a product, ask questions that will uncover the customer's decision criteria before recommending a solution. Focusing on the customer's decision criteria and not just on what you have to sell sends an important message to the customer which is vital if you are to earn their trust. The Statement of Intention Technique will help you do just that.

Statement of Intention Technique:

*"I prefer to do business with those I can completely satisfy. May I ask a few questions that will help us to very quickly determine if I can be the best possible assistance to you?"*

The seller's purpose in assisting the customer in clarifying their purchase decision criteria is so that they can determine the best possible recommendations to fulfill all of the criteria and completely satisfy the customer. When you "Know everything about your solution," as the Core Value suggest then you will ask better questions to determine customer decision criteria clarification, intended applications and their expected return on their purchase investment.

# Understanding Decision Criteria

---

**INFLUENCE QUESTION (IQ):** *What are the customer's decision criteria and priorities?*

---

As customers move forward in their purchase decisions they develop decision criteria. A relevant definition for *Purchase Decision Criteria* would be:

*Customer identified and desired factors, features or functions to be considered when purchasing a product or service that is believed to achieve some predetermined outcome.*

Many customers don't really know exactly what they want and they sometimes know even less about the variety of products or services they will consider purchasing in order to achieve it. Here's where sellers can really start to become the most assistance to their customers. While the customer may have done a degree of research, they don't always know or consider <u>all</u> of the details associated with each individual product or service choice.

Sellers are supposed to be experts in the areas of product knowledge and competitive differences. Customers may have a conceptual or general idea of what they hope to accomplish with their purchase but don't always have all of the specific decision criteria in mind when they begin moving forward with their purchase decision.

## The more tangible the criteria, the more perfect the fit!

Initial customer decision criteria can be more conceptual or intangible instead of specific and quantifiable. One example of an intangible decision criterion is when a customer says that they are unhappy with their current supplier's service. Without the insight of further clarification, they could mean a number of different things. The customer could mean that deliveries have arrived too late, there have been quality control challenges, slow call service response issues, communication breakdowns or several other things when they mention their perception of poor service. The more tangible the information about their concerns and desires the better you can fit your solution to their most important criteria.

Here are some other good reasons to make sure that all decision criteria are made tangibly quantifiable.

## Reasons for uncovering tangible decision criteria:

1. Helping the customer to more clearly define what is truly wanted or needed.

   According to customers most sellers uncover intangible decision criteria and then immediately dive into their pitch explaining how they will do a better job than the other providers. Customers don't appreciate this behavior. The jump-to-pitch selling behavior only serves to convince customers that the seller doesn't really care about them and that they don't have enough interest in understanding them. Whereas slowing down and asking questions, which help the customer more clearly define their desires, is a very differentiating way to show that your intention is to help them identify the best possible decision choice.

## 2. Better decision criteria-to-solution alignment.

Competitive offerings can appear similar. Slowing down and guiding the customer to make their decision criteria more tangible helps them differentiate one from another. Additionally, the seller will have a better idea of how to best position the value proposition of their offering and company.

## 3. Proving customer satisfaction after the sale.

In reference to our example of better service, how can you hope to prove satisfaction if you don't truly understand what the customer was unsatisfied with in the first place? The best way to create customer satisfaction is to ensure that they will be able to verify their level of satisfaction by comparing their tangible decision criteria against what was actually delivered and their achieved outcomes.

Some useful questions for making intangible decision criteria more tangible include:

- What do you mean when you say _____?
- What needs to happen for you to be completely satisfied with _____?
- What does _____ need to do for you?
- In the end, what are you trying to accomplish?
- What do you really want to achieve?
- What problems or challenges have you had with _____ in the past?
- What has caused you frustration with _____?

# Determining Decision Criteria Priorities

All customer decision criteria are not equal. Customers assign different levels of value and priority to different decision criteria. An example of this can be price. If the customer has a price decision criteria and they don't develop any criteria that has a greater level of importance, then the price becomes their number one decision priority. This is why selling value is so important.

The concept of selling value begins by asking questions which uncover additional, tangible and customer valued decision criteria. Sellers should help customers to prioritize decision criteria as it is uncovered.

Some decision criteria priority clarification questions can include:

- Which two or three of your decision criteria would you consider most important?
- Why would these criteria be important to you?
- Which of the criteria do you think is going to help you most quickly achieve the value you want to receive?
- What is most important to you?
- What is least important to you?
- What do you think other decision influencers would say are most important?
- Which of the decision criteria would you consider to be necessities?
- Which of the decision criteria would you be willing to live without?

# The Power of Three

---

**INFLUENCE QUESTION (IQ):** *What are the customer's decision criteria and priorities?*

---

As sellers ask questions to uncover the customer's current situation and motivational causes they are actually beginning to guide the customer toward refining their decision criteria and assess possible purchase choices. Because of this, the more customer improvement and repair situations sellers can uncover, the more likely the customer will perceive greater purchase value in what the seller eventually suggests.

**STRATEGY:** Always find a minimum of three ways to help the customer!

By always looking for a minimum of three ways to help every customer to improve their situation, sellers can:

- Provide better customer decision assistance.
- Curb the urge to quickly present solutions and instead, keep pace with customer decision making.
- Create more value for the customer.
- Differentiate themselves from traditional selling competitors.
- Provide the customer with the best possible product, service or solution choices.

We'll take a closer look at this concept as we address *Developing Encouraging Criteria* later in this chapter. But for now remember that before offering any purchase recommendations, sellers should always try to uncover a minimum of three ways to help their customers to improve their situation.

# DISCovery Questioning Method

Most sellers are aware of how important it is to ask questions in order to uncover customer desires, requirements and decision criteria. Unfortunately, many only ask a few questions to uncover some initial need or pain and then immediately start into their selling pitch. Sellers who do this are also jumping well ahead of the customer in their decision process. This is the most common cause of an early disconnection between the seller and the buyer during the customer's decision process.

## DISCovery Explanation

Instead, try using the *DISCovery Method* of questioning. Think of *DISCovery* as far more than a questioning procedure. It is actually a very holistic approach involving questioning, conversation and suggestions. *DISCovery* is useful when questioning an individual and can also be used when working with multiple decision influencers.

*DISCovery* creates seller and buyer conversations that follow a logically progressive path. It makes the discovery process more conversational for the customer. And according to sellers, it aids in determining whether they are meaningfully engaged with a high potential prospect. Other *DISCovery Method* outcomes include uncovering of all of the customer's decision criteria, criteria priorities and the development of the customer's perception of decision and purchase value. The *DISCovery Method* looks like this:

## DISCovery Questioning Method

| | | |
|---|---|---|
| **D** | Diagnose | *Ask questions to help the customer more clearly understand their current situation.* |
| **I** | Inform | *Share your findings and insights with the customer to determine or confirm perceptions in common.* |
| **S** | Suggest | *Offer additional recommendations which will improve the customer's situation and create the greatest value.* |
| **C** | Confirm | *Gain solution to criteria match up agreement while differentiating yourself, your company and solution.* |

## D - Diagnose

DISCovery starts with *diagnostic questions* so that sellers more clearly understand the customer's current state, situation or condition. These questions can be asked of anyone who may influence the decision but it is recommended that the seller begin by questioning the ultimate "Crucial" or final decision maker. If the Crucial Decision Maker allows the seller to speak with other decision influencers the same *DISCovery* method questions should be used with anyone the seller diagnoses.

Also, if more initial decision motivation with the *Crucial Decision Maker* is needed, then the seller should continue forward with DISC. Doing so may uncover additional decision cause motivations which can encourage the *Crucial Decision Maker* to allow the seller to speak with other decision influencers before making any recommendations.

Asking diagnostic questions should be conversational. Start by asking basic questions about what customers may want or need in a solution making sure that all of the criteria is made tangible. You may find the previously listed questions for uncovering tangible decision criteria very useful.

Then just follow the conversation where ever it may lead. Any question that sellers may ask to uncover additional cause motivations or that help to refine decision criteria would be considered a *Diagnose* question. Once the customer's situation or condition has been effectively determined then proceed to the *Inform* – *DISCovery* step.

# I - Inform

In the *DISCovery* Inform step sellers should share their findings and insights about the customer's current situation or condition and determine whether a common perspective is shared.

Just because the seller thinks that they have identified a good opportunity to improve the customer's situation that doesn't mean that the customer is in agreement. Inform is a consulting behavior. The seller talks to the *Crucial Decision Maker* and other influencers, asks questions, performs any other assessments and then shares what they believe is their understanding of the customer's situation or condition.

Consider beginning the Inform DISCovery Step with one of the following:

- Based on the information I've gathered; it appears that
  _____.

- My review of your situation/condition revealed that
  _____.

- I'd like to review my understanding of your situation...I believe we've determined that _____.

This should be followed with a question to determine to what degree the customer agrees with your findings. For example:

- Does that sound correct to you?
- Does this align with your perspective?
- Do you feel this is right?

Once the seller has shared their proposed findings and gained agreement from the customer then they should move to their next *DISCovery* step, Suggest.

# S - Suggest

The Suggest step doesn't mean that it's time to give the customer purchase recommendations. Instead the salesperson should ask additional questions that help the customer refine the possible solution recommendations. This also gives the seller the opportunity to suggest additional value enhancing criteria to the customer's list. For the customer this is a very natural and rational progression of improving their decision criteria and assessing their possible purchase options.

The Suggest *DISCovery* step creates benefits to both the customer and seller:

- The more complete the customer's list of decision criteria the more likely they will be satisfied with the results produced after their purchase.
- By making the customer aware of differentiators specific to the seller's product, the seller enhances the customer's criteria list and at the same time differentiates their proposed recommendations from the competition.

The Suggest *DISCovery* step is accomplished in two parts: Developing Encouraging Criteria and Asking Value Confirmation Questions.

## Part One: Developing Encouraging Criteria

One of the most commonly missed competitive differentiation opportunities is adding *Encouraging Criteria* to the customer's decision criteria list. Encouraging Criteria are differentiating decision criteria which have not been previously considered by the customer. This is also a wonderful opportunity to begin guiding customers toward complete satisfaction with their decision and purchase.

## Customers don't know what they don't know... you know?

Despite the wealth of information available to customers, sellers are typically more broadly knowledgeable about their products, unique applications and what their competition offers. The more knowledgeable the seller, the better they can develop Encouraging Criteria.

## New information can change old decisions!

We have all changed our minds about what to buy at one time or another because of new or additional information. The same can be said for our customers. If the seller does a great job of developing Encouraging Criteria, then several things may occur:

- The customer may become aware of additional applications for the proposed product or service.

- The seller's product may be able to fulfill criteria that the competition cannot.
- The customer may be willing to pay a premium for the seller's product / service because it can accommodate unique applications.

## STRATEGY: Ask questions to influence the customer to add Encouraging Criteria to their purchase decision criteria list!

Once the seller has identified possible *encouraging criteria* then they should ask questions to help the customer determine whether these things are important enough to add to their decision criteria list. Examples of these questions are:

## Encouraging Criteria Questions:

- Have you considered what _____ might do for you? Your company? Your team? Your customers?
- How important is it that you're able to _____?
- Do you also think that _____ is important?
- Have you ever thought about or considered _____?
- You haven't mentioned it yet, but have you ever wanted _____ to happen?
- Given the opportunity, would you also like to be able to _____?
- Have you ever heard anyone mention a need for _____?

## STRATEGY: Review the customer's situation with the eyes of a new employee!

Imagine that you were actually going to work for your customer and you are seeing their business and reviewing their current situation for the first time. As a new employee wouldn't you try to help improve their business by bringing the expertise and knowledge you've gained from your former industry? Wouldn't you try to use whatever knowledge you have to improve your new employer's environment or situation? Of course you would! Now do the same thing with all of your customers!

When sellers review their customer's situation with the eyes of a new employee they can identify opportunities for their product or service to benefit the customer in ways that had not been previously recognized.

## Part Two: Asking Value Confirmation Questions

The second part of the *DISCovery- Suggest* step is asking *Value Confirmation Questions*. Asking Value Confirmation Questions helps the customer to continue their path of self-discovery. This self-discovery helps them determine if the new criteria should be added to their purchase decision criteria list. So instead of pitching additional criteria to be considered by the customer, sellers should question the customer to aid them in discovering the value of suggested criteria.

## Value Confirmation Questions:

- Why would that be important to you?
- What issues have you dealt with in the past that might be eliminated by this?
- What could that mean to you? Your company? Your employees? Your customers?
- How would that improve your current condition?
- What could you do with _____ that you can't do now?
- What could it cost you if you don't have _____?
- If you don't have _____, what might happen?

Keep in mind that the *Suggest* step can be used repetitively to add any number of additional decision criteria to the customer's list as long as the seller remains conversational.

## C - Confirm

Customers need to feel reasonably settled on their decision criteria before they become comfortable enough to move forward with their next decision step of *Apply Decisions*. Confirm is an opportunity for sellers to insure that they are in harmony with and completely understand the decision maker's decision criteria.

## If the customer doesn't know then the sale won't go!

In many cases sellers know much more quickly than customers do what is needed to improve the customer's business and what may happen if the purchase and or changes don't occur. However, if the customer doesn't know, acknowledge or accept what the seller has already determined then the purchase decision is not moving forward.

Confirming the customer's agreement about their decision criteria and the level of importance that each holds causes them to analyze their criteria one last time and become more comfortable with them and the goals they hope to accomplish with the purchase.

This also brings closure to the customer's Assess Options buying decision step and propels them forward in their decision process.

# Confirmation Questions

The following is an easily implemented positioning approach used to confirm the customer's decision criteria and priorities:

## STRATEGY: Position for confirmation and then Confirm

*"It is important to me that you are completely satisfied with any decision you make. To ensure that goal is realized, I'd like us to take a step back for a moment and review what we know so far so that we can verify that you're on track to make the best possible decision. Would that be O.K.?"*

This is an easy way to make sure that the seller remains connected to the customer's decision process and at the same time differentiate themselves as truly customer-centric! According to customers when sellers slow down, confirm customer criteria and remain in-sync with their decision speed they appreciate this differentiating behavior.

Once properly positioned then some useful confirmation questions are:

- Of the decision criteria we've discussed which two or three are most important to you... and why?
- Which would you say are least important... and why?
- Which criteria do you believe are imperative in achieving your goals?
- Have any of your criteria priorities "shifted" up or down during our discussions... and why?
- To your knowledge, is there anyone else involved in this decision that might prioritize these criteria differently?

- In the future as you look back on this decision how will you know for sure that it was a success?
- Do you have any concerns or thoughts that we haven't discussed?

# Wrapping Up DISCovery

Remember that DISCovery is a method of questioning, generating meaningful conversation and developing important decision criteria recommendations. It should be used with any decision influencer that the seller has the opportunity to engage.

Sellers will find that *DISCovery* is more easily accomplished if they are well prepared. In preparation for using *DISCovery* it is recommended that sellers consider the following as part of their preparation when asking and answering their influence question, *"How can I increase the customer's perception of differentiated value in me, my company and solution?"*

## DISCovery Preparation Considerations

1. In what three ways I might be able to improve the customer's situation or condition?
2. Which *Diagnose* step questions might I use?
3. Which *Inform* approach might I be most comfortable using with this customer?
4. Are there any *Encouraging Criteria* that I might suggest?
5. What questions might I ask the customer to uncover the *Encouraging Criteria*?
6. Which *Value Confirmation* question do I think I will be most comfortable using?

If sellers will consider using these preparation questions as part of their meeting or discussion preparation I'm sure that they will be much more conversational in their approach and they will certainly differentiate themselves from most of their competitors.

# Information, Applications and Outcomes

As with most educational experiences this book provides the reader with information which they may not have previously possessed. New information is always good for stimulating new ideas and can sometimes help to reshape our perceptions and behavior. But in order for the information to have the best chance of being effectively used, the transition from information to application must occur.

Please consider taking the time to answer the provided questions in order to begin your own information to application transition. These transitions will help to guarantee the fastest and most useful applications and outcomes in your selling career.

*What Information was provided in this chapter that you felt was important and possible useful to you?*

*How might you apply these important points of information?*

*What outcomes do you hope or expect to produce as a result of your application implementations?*

Chapter Eight:

# Align Solution

# Decision Influence Step Three: Align Solution

*Align Solution* is the third *Influence Step.* Let's review the goals of this step:

The Align Solution - Influence Step goals are:

- Know everything about the competition.
- Know everything about their company and solution.
- Continue to gain competitive advantage.
- Deliver effective purchase decision recommendations (by presentation if necessary).
- If required, negotiate to mutually beneficial conclusion.
- Confirm agreement and secure the customer partnership.

The *Influence Questions* (IQ) and customer Internal Questions alignment for the seller's *Align Solution* and the customer's *Apply Decisions* steps are:

| Seller Influence Questions for Align Solution | Customer Internal Questions for Apply Decisions |
|---|---|
| • What can I do to best align our solution with the customer's decision criteria?<br>• Why should the customer do business with us and not the competition?<br>• How can we confirm agreement without confrontation? | • Am I still comfortable with my decision criteria?<br>• Have I considered all of the available decision options and chosen the one that is best for me?<br>• Do I still perceive enough value to move forward in making the decision? |

Once the seller and customer have a clear understanding of the customer's prioritized buying decision, it becomes time for the seller to move to their next *Decision Influence Step - Align Solution*. Remember that at this point, the customer will soon be asking and answering their Apply Decisions internal questions shown above. Sellers should continue to guide customers by answering their influence questions.

## *The journey is easier when the path is clear!*

If the seller has done a great job in their last influence step of *Refine Criteria, then* the customer will have affirmatively answered their last *Assess Options* internal question *"Do I still perceive enough value to proceed forward with my decision?"* Now it is time to guide the customer through their *Apply Decisions* buying decision step.

Making sure that the recommended solution is completely aligned with the buyer's decision criteria is critical. This influence step is also important in finally eliminating any competition from the decision maker's list of possible purchase choices.

# Criteria to Solution Alignment

*The only "perfect" solution is the one which aligns "perfectly" with the customer's decision criteria!*

---

**INFLUENCE QUESTION (IQ):** *What can I do to best align our solutions with the customer's decision criteria?*

---

In the customer's *Apply Decisions* buying decision step they attempt to answer the internal question, *"Have I considered all of the available decision options and chosen the one that is best for me?"*

Many sellers have previously believed that their product and value proposition presentation is what caused customers to become motivated and buy. As a result, they have taken the first available opportunity to present what they have to sell. They have hoped that one or more of the features, functions, applications or benefits might entice their prospects into buying. This is why the "canned" presentation became so popular among sellers and their managers.

Based on the things we've discussed so far; this is obviously an unproductive tactic. As was explained in the previous influence steps, customer perceptions of value are created much earlier in their decision process. And as sellers refine the customer's decision criteria though questioning, the decision maker perceptions of value can be enhanced.

I completely agree that salespeople should know everything about what they have to sell. In fact, the *Cooperation Selling - Core Value* of *"Know everything about your solution"* suggests that product and application knowledge is a primary seller responsibility.

But the true intention for this knowledge should be to more effectively question and educate decision makers to guide them and discern what they really need. This will then help customers to determine which offering they believe is their best purchase choice.

## More information helps the customer to make a more informed decision!

So the purpose of knowing everything about their solution is so that the sellers can do a better job of:

1. Determining the customer's current condition or situation.
2. Aligning with decision influencers to guide them through their decision process.
3. Determining influencers and decision maker's decision criteria and their priorities for those criteria.
4. Adding encouraging criteria to influencer and decision maker criteria lists.
5. Clarifying the final recommended offering so that the best solution to criteria alignment is created.

## Solution recommendations should begin as a one-to-one solution to criteria alignment!

The last in this list, "*Clarify the final recommended offering so that the best solution to criteria alignment is created*" provides sellers with an opportunity to confirm solution differentiation and settle the customer into their final purchase option choice. This is accomplished by reviewing the customer's criteria list and then sharing with them how the seller's proposed offering will fulfill all of their decision criteria.

# Competitive Positioning

---

**INFLUENCE QUESTION (IQ):** *Why should the customer do business with us and not the competition?*

---

Solution-to-decision criteria alignment plays a critical role in creating a competitive advantage. If the seller has partnered with the customer to effectively refine their decision criteria, especially with the addition of *encouraging criteria,* then they are best competitively positioned as the customer moves forward. But, how can the salesperson be sure that they are in the best possible competitive position?

Every seller has wondered if they were in the strongest competitive position with a decision maker. And when a seller is unsure about their competitive position it can be stressful. This stress can, in turn, cause sellers to transmit their concern and apprehension to their customer. The seller may even undervalue their own recommendations by offering discounts which can also easily undermine their work toward value creation.

# Developing a Differentiation Statement

Using the Cooperation Selling™ methodology changes the buying experience for the better.

Despite that, you may still be required to competitively differentiate yourself above and beyond your product. Even though your customer may be comparing your offering to their decision criteria and to the competition, they still may be asking "Why should I do business with your company?" or "Why should I do business with you rather than the competition?" It is important that if a customer asks these questions that the seller is prepared to communicate their uniqueness and differentiation.

Unfortunately, when sellers are not proactively prepared to effectively answer the uniqueness question they tend to say things like, "Well, you get me!" Then they begin to explain why buying from them is better because the customer can count on them! This response means very little to most customers because they've been disappointed by other sellers who have told them the same thing. Besides, if this is what most unprepared sellers have said in the past then it really isn't very unique, is it?

## STRATEGY: Create your Differentiation Statement

To create the most valid differentiation statement sellers should start by listing all of the competitive advantages they believe they, their company and their products offer. Once this list is complete then sellers should distill their list by considering the following question:

*What do your customers truly want and need that you, your company and/or your solution do better than your competition?*

If sellers will consider what they believe their competitive advantages are and then use those advantages to discern the answer to this question, then they are well on their way to creating a true differentiation statement. This differentiation statement becomes the best answer to the customer question, "Why should I do business with you?"

# Creating Competitive Differentiation

*The customer has decision criteria and priorities. The offering which best fits their criteria and priorities is the one that they choose!*

Sellers should understand that customer competitive decision making is not arbitrary. The customer has decision criteria and priorities for each criterion. They either developed their criteria and priorities on their own or with someone's help. When the time comes to make their final purchase decision, the offering they choose is commonly the one that most closely aligns with their decision criteria and their priorities.

**STRATEGY:** Analyze your solution alignment and competitive position.

Should sellers want to determine where they really stand at any given time in a competitive selling situation then they should consider using the following analytic steps to determine their true competitive position.

## Step One: List the customer's tangible decision criteria and priorities.

Create a list of all of the customer's decision criteria and what you believe are the customer's priorities for each criterion. Remember that the customer will use these criteria and priorities to navigate their purchase decision choices and discern which choice option is best for them. So begin by creating a customer criteria list and then prioritize that list the way they think the customer would.

## Step Two: Compare the known competitors and their abilities.

Once the criteria list is complete; then the seller should use their competitive knowledge to determine which competitor has the advantage in most effectively delivering on each of the customer's individual decision criteria. Obviously the more product and competitive knowledge you possess the easier it will be to analyze your ability to deliver against the competitor's ability to deliver on each criterion.

## Step Three: Consider the customer's priorities for each of their decision criteria

Now if you review what you believe the customer's priorities for each of the listed decision criteria then you should be able to discern which competitive solution the customer is most likely to choose.

*Customers are more likely to choose the solution which best aligns with their decision criteria and priorities!*

This solution alignment and competitive position exercise (commonly called a Competitive Analysis) is one of the easiest ways for sellers to determine where they really stand in the hierarchy of customer choice preference.

When sellers think of solution development in this context it helps them to begin differentiating their solution earlier by uncovering or discovering "Encouraging Criteria" during their customer's *Assess Options* buying decision step. By the way, if sellers understand and use this method of determining their competitive selling position it will go a long way in helping them realize why they win or lose deals when competing for sales.

# Commonly Missed Differentiation Opportunities

Differentiation is critical in competitive situations. Unfortunately, what many sellers don't understand is that several differentiation opportunities are created early in the customer buying decision process. This is one of the common reasons why so many sellers find themselves frustrated when the competitive offering is chosen.

If the seller didn't differentiate by changing the customer experience early in the engagement, then product differentiation may not be enough to sway the customer's final purchase choice. So it is critically important for sellers to differentiate themselves earlier in the customer's buying decision process. Let's consider some of the most commonly missed seller differentiation opportunities:

- ✓ Act differently by:
  - Differentiating your selling approach from traditional sellers.
  - Focusing on the customer and their decision process, not the close.
  - Caring about the customer and guiding them do what is best for them is a tremendous differentiator.
- ✓ Ask more questions and listen to the answers.
- ✓ Slow down and match your influence and selling efforts to the customer's chosen decision speed. This encourages

the customer to feel more *guided* rather than *pushed* toward a decision.

✓ Dig deeper for tangible, prioritized and encouraging decision criteria. Make sure that a customer's decision criteria list is complete, quantifiable and prioritized.

✓ Question to add encouraging criteria to the customer's list. This will create a differentiated solution opportunity.

✓ Confirm Customer Expectations by making sure that the proposed solution is the best possible fit with the customer's expectations.

## *Sales are lost much more frequently because of a lack of perceived value than they are because of price.*

We often hear sellers blame the loss of a sale on the lower price of a competitor. That might be the case when price is the highest priority decision making criteria. However, in many cases, customer simply perceived more *value* in the competitive offering.

Everyone has heard, "It's not about price it's about value!" But too many sellers think that this means the more features, functions, applications and benefits they present, the greater the value.

We should better understand by now that this is not what the axiom really means. How it *should* be interpreted is that the more value the customer perceives then the more motivated they are to purchase and the more they may be willing to pay. Value is created by using the *Cooperative Selling*™ methodology and strategies to differentiate your offerings and closely aligning your features, benefits and applications to your customer's higher prioritized buying criteria.

When the customer recognizes the potential for greater value achievement then they will sometimes spend more for a product in order to achieve it. Although this doesn't mean that if a seller does all of the right things that they will never lose a competitive sale over price. If one of the customer's higher priority decision criteria happens to be price and other differentiated but lower prioritized criteria don't offer enough combined value, then the customer may simply choose the lower priced option. But what it does mean is that if a seller sells the *Cooperation Selling*™ way then their closing percentage will improve and they will lose fewer sales to the price criterion choice.

# Navigating "Late Entry" Engagements

One selling challenge that is frequently asked about is how to handle "Late Entry" engagements. The most common examples of Late Entry engagement are situations where the customer reaches out to the provider with a Request for Proposal *(RFP)* or Request for Quote *(RFQ)*.

These can be challenging because by the time the customer reaches out to the seller most *Crucial Decision Makers:*

- Have already developed what they believe are their purchase decision criteria.
- Have probably worked with an incumbent or competitive seller to develop their criteria.
- Are well downstream in their buying decision process; normally in their *Assess Options* or *Apply Decisions* buying decision step.

- May be simply attempting to justify a purchase decision they believe they have already completed.
- May have pushed the decision down to the *Support Level* of decision making for fulfillment.
- Could simply be price shopping.

Whatever the real story, many sellers say that this is a difficult, consistently unrewarding and precarious situation to be in. In fact according to sellers who find themselves in the late engagement situation, the common selling outcomes are:

- A low percentage of completed sales when compared to the number of presentations and proposals they must produce.
- Fewer opportunities to speak with *Leadership Tier* decision makers.
- A lesser or reduced profit margin in the sales that are actually completed.
- More adversarial friction and customer communicated push back.

No doubt, these outcomes identify the late engagement as one of the more difficult situations to navigate and yet according to sellers, their companies frequently expect them to pursue these opportunities with equal passion, commitment and time as they might any other.

## *Just because it is difficult that doesn't mean that it cannot be accomplished!*

I certainly understand why companies would not want a late engagement disqualified as an opportunity just because the seller finds this situation difficult to navigate. But on the other hand I can understand seller's frustrations. From the seller's perspective it takes a lot of time to respond to the RFP or RFQ and the actual reward versus time invested may appear to be less than productive. So what should salespeople do when they face the Late Entry engagement?

## STRATEGY: "GO-BACK" in the decision process for more influence and better results!

Your best chance in these situations is to have the customer walk you through their decision process. This gives you the opportunity to ask questions to uncover more customer goals and criteria that may give you the competitive edge. Here is how to do that:

## Go-Back Step One: Suggest that you will only engage if you are sure you can help.

If the seller did not help the customer originally determine their decision criteria, then they cannot be sure that their proposed offering will completely satisfy the customer. In fact, it is safe to assume that the customer may not have developed a complete decision criteria list.

So the salesperson's first step is to suggest that they will only engage if they are sure they can *completely satisfy* the customer. This means that the seller really needs the opportunity to talk to the decision maker or influencers who developed the decision criteria.

Gaining permission and entry to those who developed the decision criteria can become more difficult the further down the decision tier ladder that sellers finds themselves when initially engaged. If you recall the *Producer Tier's* concerns are things like:

✓ Fulfilling Daily Job Requirements.
✓ Following Standard Operating Procedures.
✓ Adhering to Management and Leadership Directives.
✓ Not Making Mistakes.
✓ Achieving Shorter-Term Goals.
✓ Maintaining Spending Budgets.

So if the purchase decision criteria were developed by a decision maker or influencer in the *Management or Leadership Tiers* then persuading the *Producer Tier* decision influencer to introduce the seller to their managers and leaders can be quite challenging. There are three recommended best practice approaches for accomplishing this task:

## Best Practice #1: Be honest about the situation.

If the seller shares with the *Producer Tier* influencer their true concerns about not being able to completely satisfying the customer, then that is sometimes enough to help the producer understand why the seller should talk to their supervisors. The seller should explain honestly that they only wish to do business with those customers who they believe they can completely satisfy. Because they didn't have the opportunity to help develop the original decision criteria they cannot be sure that several important criteria weren't overlooked or left out. So the seller would like the opportunity to question those who developed the decision criteria because they want to ask questions that might help discover whether additional or different decision criteria should be considered to amend the customer's original criteria list.

*Best Practice #2: Present the collection of more information as a Producer benefit.*

If the *Producer Tier* influencer purchases a less than effective product, then they may be asked by supervisors to justify their purchase choice. If the seller suggests that they can help the producer eliminate any purchase mistakes by asking a few questions of the right people, then the producer may be inclined to allow the them to gain access to those who created the criteria. This could be of great benefit for their company and could cause the producer to look good to their supervisors as well.

NOTE: *Recognize that even though both of these approaches are proven to work that they may not always work. So if the seller cannot influence the Producer to connect them with those who developed the decision criteria then there is one more way to get a few more questions answered.*

## Best Practice #3: Request for the producer to ask the questions.

As long as the seller is selective with the questions they would like answered then they may consider asking the Producer to go to the appropriate influencers or decision maker and ask questions for them prior to the seller's RFP or RFQ response. Besides, if the questions the seller asks uncovers additional criteria or even better encouraging criteria, then the seller may find themselves in a conversation with the decision maker or greater influencers anyway.

## Go-Back Step Two: Use the *Uncover Opportunity* influence step to help decision makers uncover more motivation and gain their trust

When the seller does get to speak with decision influencers then they should start by going back to their *Uncover Opportunity* influence step. Just as if the seller had started with the customer in their *Acquire Information* buying decision step, they should ask questions that uncover the motivation behind the customer's original reason for considering the purchase decision. The seller should also ask questions that might uncover additional motivational cause. This can drive customer confidence and possibly elevate the seller to more of a *Trusted Advisor* status.

## Go-Back Step Three: Use the *DISCovery* method in the Refine Criteria influence step to uncover additional decision motivation and encouraging criteria.

Using the *DISCovery* questions will aid sellers in uncovering additional customer decision criteria that otherwise may not have been considered. It also provides the opportunity for uncovering encouraging criteria which can alter the customer's decision criteria list and may possibly differentiate the seller's recommended solution.

Unfortunately, there is no single technique that will completely eliminate the Late Entry issue or the *Producer Tier* behavior. But using these three steps will provide many additional conversation and questioning opportunities. Top producing sellers recommend that these three steps should be attempted prior to making the decision to respond to the request for quote or to disengage.

# Presentation Best Practices

*The purpose of a recommendation presentation is to help customers link their decision criteria to the proposed solution, applications and outcomes!*

In many industries it is common practice for sellers to present final offering or solution recommendations prior to asking for the customer's business. But there are also other reasons to consider presentation best practices. Sellers actually do customer presentations for several reasons.

## Presentation Motives

✓ Offering information to the customer which should aid them in their buying decision process.

✓ Demonstrating useful applications which may be considered as decision criteria.

✓ Sharing and acquiring relevant information with *Decision Influence Groups.*

✓ Helping the customer to explore possible decision criteria options.

✓ Recommendations of proposed offerings or solutions.

But the real purpose of any of these presentations is to help customers link their decision criteria to the proposed solution, applications and outcomes. If sellers wish to make their presentations most useful and valuable then there are three presentation components which should be considered: *Preparation, Organization and Delivery.*

# Presentation Preparation Before Organization

*Cooperation Selling*™ sellers understand that you rarely get a second chance to do a great presentation and because of this they spend much more time strategizing and preparing for their presentation than they do organizing and delivering it.

## *Preparation propels presentation performance!*

When examining how great sellers prepare for a presentation, several important preparation questions begin to emerge. It is recommended that these presentation preparation questions should be used as a simple checklist in order to drive enhanced presentation delivery and performance.

## Presentation Preparation Checklist:

- ✓ Who will be attending the meeting?
- ✓ What role does each influencer play in the overall decision process?
- ✓ Have you prepared a collaborative list of all decision influencer decision criteria?
- ✓ Are you comfortable and confident with the solution you are recommending?
- ✓ Will your proposed solution fulfill all of the customer's decision criteria and goals?
- ✓ How will the customer's decision criteria and goals be clearly stated and addressed?
- ✓ Have you developed an attention gathering opening for your presentation?
- ✓ How will you communicate your differentiated value?

✓ Have you prepared a list of questions that will engage the customer and create two-way conversation?

✓ Are you aware of and are you prepared to manage any opposing influence?

✓ Have you prepared your presentation to present the best possible solution to criteria alignment?

✓ Do you possess comprehensive knowledge of your proposed solution's applications and possible customer benefits?

✓ Do you possess enough competitive information and knowledge?

✓ Do you feel comfortable with the solution price and the value perception you've helped to create for the customer?

✓ Will you be providing a profit improvement, expected value or expected return on investment summary?

✓ Are any team presentation goals or roles established and aligned to work most effectively with members of the Decision Influence Group?

✓ What objections might be raised and how will you overcome them?

✓ What questions might be asked and how will you respond to them?

✓ If you intend to ask for the business or partnership, what are your negotiation guidelines?

✓ Are you prepared to negotiate anything other than price, rate or investment?

✓ Are there any concessions you are willing to offer instead of a discount?

✓ How will you ask for the partnership or business?

✓ Six months from now how should the customer measure purchase success and how will you explain this?

# Presentation Organization

The *Presentation Preparation Checklist* is a great way to make sure that sellers have most of the information they will need to organize a powerful presentation. Asking and answering the checklist questions will prepare sellers to give more potent presentations because they will think more deeply about the customer's purchase decision criteria, other influencers who may be involved in the decision and their own abilities and knowledge.

Organizing the presentation will settle sellers into a determined agenda and narrow their focus. Remember that you may have the best solution in the world but you must also be capable of communicating the components and value to the customer in an effective way and in the proposed time frame.

## Presentation Organization Best Practices:

1.  Determine how much time the customer will allot for the presentation. *The best practice recommendation is to prepare to deliver the presentation in 50% of the allotted time and leave 50% of the time for questions, answers and discussion.*

2.  Determine who will be attending the presentation, each influencer's decision criteria and the level of influence and credibility each has with the *Crucial Decision Maker*. (*More information about Decision Influence Group member influence and credibility is reviewed in the Selling To Decision Influence Groups chapter.*)

3.  Review, rehearse and time the *criteria-to-solution alignment* portion of the presentation. The criteria-to-solution alignment creates greater perceptions of value for each decision influencer.

4. Reiterate any value the customer has already communicated as important. Make sure that customers know they will be receiving what they have already deemed as important.

5. Determine any questions that you might ask to validate purchase decision criteria and increase decision influencer participation. Participation increases influencer buy-in, ownership of the proposed offering and adaptability motivation for after purchase implementation.

6. Consider the possible questions which may be asked of you and the objections which may be posed. Determine how to best answer the questions and respond to the objections.

# Presentation Delivery

Following a few simple presentation delivery guidelines should ensure that the seller's recommendations are more likely to be understood, valued and accepted by their customers. A recommendation presentation should be a one-to-one solution to criteria alignment, an opportunity for the seller to respond to questions and objections, possible negotiation and hopefully the finalization of critical purchase agreements.

## Presentation Delivery Recommendations:

1. Prepare and offer a meeting agenda.

   People like to know in advance how their time is going to be invested in a meeting. Sellers should settle customers into the presentation meeting by sharing what should be expected over the course of the meeting.

2. Always ask "Has anything changes since we last spoke?"

   Not asking this question can cause sellers to find out that what they are proposing no longer fits the customer's decision criteria or preferred outcomes. It is far better to be aware of changes that have occurred and possibly tailor proposed recommendations on the fly.

3. Be prepared to listen and make appropriate adjustments.

   In the process of making their purchase decision, customers may need to respond to changes or new information. If the customer's decision criteria change then the offering may also need to change in some way. Remember that the goal is to completely satisfy the customer.

4. Never speak in terms or jargon the customer may not understand.

   Sellers should never risk confusing customers with industry terms or jargon that may make it more difficult for the customer to listen, participate or understand.

5. Present all of the decision criteria to solution alignments first and then review any additional features, applications or benefits which might be useful to the customer.

   *NOTE: If the seller starts talking about things that the customer has not already determined are important then they run the risk of convincing the customer that they weren't listening or don't care. Worse yet, this behavior can easily be associated with traditional selling salespeople who simply pitch without regard for the customer, their decision criteria or their decision process. It's ok to share additional useful information with the customer about the solution or providing*

company but first deliver the criteria to solution alignment
and then ask for permission to share additional information.

Here's an example:

"Now that we've reviewed how these recommendations match
what we've together determined you want and need, would you
mind if I shared a little additional information that I think you'll
also find important?"

6. Be proactively prepared to negotiate.

   *Most sellers know that the greater the customer's percep-*
   *tion of value, the less likely they are to negotiate. But that*
   *doesn't mean that sellers should not prepare in case the*
   *customer does want to negotiate. Here are 5 questions to*
   *answer in order to prepare for a potential negotiation:*

   ✓ Are you confident that you've done all of the right
   things?
   ✓ Is there any other possible value you might guide the
   customer to uncover?
   ✓ What could you offer the customer that would improve
   your position with them?
   ✓ What concessions are you willing to give in order to
   complete this sale?
   ✓ Do you know what your negotiation top and bottom are?

7. Determine how you will ask for the business or partnership.

At some point the seller will need to ask for their customer
to purchase. Being unprepared or unrehearsed will send
the wrong message. In fact, according to surveyed decision makers, if the seller doesn't ask them to purchase

then decision makers may feel like the seller is not confident that their recommendation is the best one.

# Conditioning Expectations and Commitments

In order to do more business and completely satisfy the largest number of customers, sellers must strive to eliminate the possibility of misunderstandings. If the customer decides to move forward with their purchase decision it is critical that both the seller and decision maker have a concise understanding of what is to be expected from and delivered by both parties. To guarantee customer satisfaction and eliminate misunderstandings:

✓ Make sure expectations are clear and fulfilled to build trust.

Buying and selling can require several conversations and communications. During those communications commitments may be made by either or both parties. Sellers should close the loop on any prior commitments to the customer before asking the for their purchase decision. If sellers desire their customer's trust and desire to move forward confidently in their partnership, then the customer must feel that the seller can be trusted to keep all of their commitments.

✓ Make sure all decision criteria and expectations are tangible.

The concept of digging deeper and asking more questions to ensure that all decision criteria are made tangible was reviewed in the previous Refine Criteria influence step chapter. As you probably recall, one of the reasons for making sure that all of the customer's decision criteria are made tangible is so that satisfaction can be proven after the sale.

But there may other expectations which customers may need fulfilled. The seller should make any additional expectations as tangible as possible as well. Additional customer expectations might include:

- Delivery dates.
- Promised and provided training.
- Inter-company introductions.
- Service scheduling.
- Financing terms.
- And many others which may occur as a natural course of doing business.

Sellers should ensure that any promises they've made or any expectations the customer may have of them or their company have been clearly defined so that those expectations can be fulfilled and proven.

✓  Put everything in writing.

Sellers should make sure that any proposed recommendations are supported by documentation in order to prevent miscommunications or misunderstandings. It is not enough to tell the customer that something will be taken care of. Sellers should make written notes of any promises that they or their customers make so that both parties eventually feel satisfied that those promises have been reasonably fulfilled. The MOI or Message of Intent discussed in the Uncover Opportunity influence step chapter is an excellent mechanism for making sure that any commitments by either party are recorded and fulfilled.

# Obtaining Critical Agreements

---

**INFLUENCE QUESTION (IQ):** *How can we confirm agreements without confrontation?*

---

*The goal of Cooperation Selling is to harmonize the intentions, motivations and actions of the provider and customer.*

This concept should certainly extend to what has been for so long referred to as 'closing.' We've all heard customers criticize sellers about their aggressive behaviors or techniques when closing. These complaints suggest that customers don't really care for the hard sell and hard close selling approaches. And yet, I've also overheard sellers and their supervisors rave about a salesperson's ability to "Slam the door and get the deal!" This appears to be a conflict of selling and buying motivations.

*Salespeople don't close more business by focusing on closing; they close more business by focusing on the customer!*

The very nature of congratulating salespeople for their hard sell or hard close approach suggests that someone is putting way too much emphasis on closing. Please don't misunderstand. All sellers hope to secure the sale. But assigning too much importance to the close is a common byproduct of being too focused on the selling process or the sale and not focused enough on the buyer and their decision process.

When I bring up focusing on the buyer and their decision process instead of the sale in sales training classes I've actually had sellers and even some managers say, "Don't you understand? I've got a quota to achieve every month! I've got to focus on closing!"

## *The shortcut to the number has always been the customer!*

The pressure to sell and close exists. But in order to best accomplish their selling goals sellers should better understand where good sales come from and what they should actually do in order to generate more of them. Sellers need to put themselves in the best possible selling position by focusing on guiding their customers through their decision process and always keeping a full selling funnel or pipeline.

## *Great sellers always have a full selling funnel or pipeline!*

When a seller's sales funnel (or pipeline) is empty, the seller may feel inclined to apply more closing pressure with less regard for the benefit of the customer. In essence, the seller becomes more aggressive when closing because of the concern they have about achieving their selling goals and because they have too few prospects in their pipeline to comfortably accomplish their goals. With a full pipeline, the seller knows that they have many other selling opportunities which promotes a focus on the entire influence process and not just the close.

## *Selling success comes easiest when you do the right things...every day!*

The "right things" for some sellers might mean a better and more frequently achieved prospecting plan. For those who have more account management type selling responsibilities the "right things" might mean working every day to get higher, wider and deeper into their customer organizations. It could also mean frequently looking for changes that would offer additional selling opportunities to their current customer list. But whatever the seller's selling responsibilities, they should always try to produce the daily activities that will put a greater number of the right, qualified prospects into their selling funnel or pipeline. This is the only way that sellers can achieve their selling objectives and always feel free to remain focused on doing what is best for the customer.

# Positioning Critical Agreements

Many sellers fear asking for a purchase commitment. In fact, our experience with sellers suggests the following:

*The number one reason that sellers don't complete the sale is because they don't ask for the business!*

Consider this; the seller has been asking for commitments from the beginning of the engagement when he or she asked, "Is this a good time to talk?" Asking for the business is just one more question along the way.

Asking for the business is not in itself an act of aggression or confrontation. In fact, the opposite can be true. By asking for the business the seller is actually guiding the customer to answer their third *Apply Decisions* step internal question, *"Do I still perceive enough value to move forward with the decision?"*

A purchase decision is a conscious choice. By asking for the business sellers are signaling to the customer that the time has come for them to consciously choose to review their previous decision efforts and move forward toward a decisive conclusion. This is just the next rational and natural step in their decision process.

Let's try to eliminate the undue pressure that many sellers experience when it becomes time to close or ask for the business. I've witnessed good salespeople go into "closing shock" because of the pressure they put on themselves to find the perfect closing question or approach. I believe that much of this concern occurs because the seller is not completely sure how the decision maker is going to react. To some degree it does matter how the seller asks. But, how the seller asks for the business is not nearly as important as how they have behaved before they ask.

*Prove to customers your good intentions with Cooperation Selling™ behavior and then ask confidently for the business.*

Prior to asking for the business, the Cooperation Selling™ seller has shown the customer their true intentions. By now the seller should have displayed through their behavior that they are different from other salespeople and that their intention is to partner with the customer in making their best possible decision. Once the customer understands the seller's helping intentions then the seller can ask for the business in almost any fashion and the customer will probably not perceive them as aggressive or manipulative.

# Creating a "Win – Win" Situation

There has been much discussion over the years about creating a "win – win" situation with the customer when selling. I have asked both sellers and sales managers in training classes to define or explain what win-win actually means. In response to this question I've heard things like, "both parties must be satisfied"; "both parties must get what they want"; "both parties must give and receive" and several other examples which probably express the concept of win-win but really don't explain what must happen if the win-win situation is actually going to occur. We must dig a little deeper in order to truly understand what a win-win really is. Consider the following as a deeper and better defined explanation of a win-win situation.

## A Win for the Customer:

For the customer to consider the purchase to be a win they must believe that all of their tangible decision criteria have been identified and will be fulfilled in what they believe is a reasonable time frame. If the customer is not comfortable with their decision criteria, if they don't believe that the criteria can lead to their complete satisfaction or if they don't receive what they believe they were promised as a result of their purchase, then they will not be satisfied regardless of the price they pay.

## A Win for the Seller:

For the seller to perceive a win on their side of the equation then they must acquire the sale or partnership, maintain what the company believes is a reasonable margin of profit and achieve closure on any promises made by the customer. Think about it. If the seller sells but doesn't maintain the profit margin expected by their company or if the new customer doesn't fulfill all their promises to the seller and the providing company then it really wasn't a winning sale for the seller.

Far too many situations occur where sales were completed but either the seller or buyer were not satisfied with the outcome because these win-win criteria were not fulfilled. The best practice strategy that should be considered and followed to create the greatest number of win-win situations is:

## STRATEGY: Sell with the end in mind!

This means that sellers should keep in mind the win-win condition they want to create. If a seller sells the way *Cooperation Selling*™ suggests then the probability of producing the win-win situation is much more likely to occur. So sellers should sell and behave the way *Cooperation Selling*™ suggests and with the win-win situation end in mind!

# Asking for The Business or Partnership

As was mentioned earlier the most common reason that sellers don't obtain the critical agreement of purchase or partnership is because they don't ask. We've explored why sellers don't always feel comfortable enough to ask and what they can do to put themselves in the most comfortable and confident position before asking. *So how* should sellers ask for the business or partnership and what should they do if their customer attempts to negotiate. Let's review some best practice ways of asking for the customer to purchase.

*Prove to customers your helpful and differentiated intentions with Cooperation Selling™ values and behavior. Then ask confidently for their business.*

There are three best practice approaches recommended for asking for the customer's business:

- ✓ Matter of Fact Approach
- ✓ Criteria Stack Approach
- ✓ Compelling Reason Approach

Let's review these three approaches to create a better understanding of each.

## The Matter of Fact Approach

*(State factually the next steps for both you and the customer.)*

Example:

*"Service will begin for you on Monday. You'll need to choose a password and sign in on our website and as we discussed. I'll set up your billing for the 15th of each month. Does that sound acceptable?"*

This *Matter of Fact* approach is very similar to the recommendations suggested for obtaining *Cooperation Commitments* and is frequently used by sellers who consistently ask for and obtain *Cooperation Commitments*. Customers can become very comfortable with this approach if sellers consistently ask for *Cooperation Commitments* during the engagement. As a result of the seller asking for multiple *Cooperation Commitments* over the course of the engagement decision makers are probably expecting the seller to ask for a final decision commitment. Using a familiar approach with the customer can actually make it easier for them to say yes.

## The Criteria Stack Approach

*(Combine and explain the decision criteria which have been previously uncovered and agreed upon.)*

Example:

*"You mentioned that _____ was important to you. You also said that _____ and _____ were essential if you were to move forward with your decision. Since you and I both agree that our (product/service) will accomplish all of these things for you, is there any reason why we shouldn't go forward?"*

With the *Criteria Stack* approach the seller is simply confirming what they and their customer already believe to be true. Reviewing or restating some of the customer's higher prioritized criteria and reminding them of the solution to criteria alignment is often enough to gain their critical agreement to purchase.

## The Compelling Reason Approach

*(State what the customer communicated is the most important reason(s) or motivational cause(s) for making the purchase decision.)*

Example:

*"Since we both agree that this is the best solution for achieving your productivity improvement goals... shall we complete this purchase for you?"*

Of the three recommended best practice approaches the *Compelling Reason* approach is probably the easiest one for sellers to use. This assumes that the seller has uncovered all of the customer's tangible decision criteria, completed a great criterion to solution alignment and guided the customer to answer all of their internal questions so far in their decision process. This approach often creates the easiest path to a "yes."

## Verifying Agreement Questions

You may have noticed that each of the three best practice approaches used to ask for the business end with a question to verify the agreement. It is always recommended that sellers verify their customer's agreement by asking a verifying agreement question. Some examples of recommended *Verifying Agreement* questions are:

✓ Do you see any reason why we shouldn't go forward?
✓ Doesn't that make sense?
✓ Don't you agree?
✓ Does that sound acceptable?
✓ Shall we complete this for you?
✓ Are we ready to move forward?

# Objections, Questions and Negotiations

*Objections are really nothing more than questions or concerns that may arise as decision makers attempt to ask and answer their internal decision making questions.*

According to many salespeople, handling or overcoming customer objections is one of their least favorite selling responsibilities. It is easy to understand why they might feel this way. Traditional selling methodologies have positioned the seller and customer in a somewhat adversarial provider-customer circumstance. Given that, sellers may feel that objections are battles that have to be won if they are going to sell. Let's try to shift our perceptions.

*Cooperation Selling*™ sellers know that objections are really nothing more than questions or concerns that arise for the customer as they attempt to ask and answer their internal decision making questions. An analysis into why decision makers raise objections has revealed that there are two basic types of objections. These two types are Rational objections and Emotional objections.

✓ Rational Objections

Rational objections commonly occur when the customer does not perceive enough value in the recommended purchase or in making the purchase decision. Rational objections may surface as either questions or objections.

✓ Emotional Objections

Emotional objections most commonly occur when the customer feels emotional distress over the possible negative consequences of making the decision. Emotional objections may surface as irrational questions or objections.

# Managing Rational Objections

One of the best ways to manage and overcome rational objections is to use the *Courtesy, Cause and Commitment* approach.

Courtesy: Show courtesy by listening to the question or stated issue and restate what was heard to the customer so they know that you understand. As an example, if the customer says something like, "I'm not sure this is something that I really need." Then the seller should show the decision maker courtesy by initially responding with something like:

*"So you are concerned because you're not quite sure that this is something you really need to have right now. Is that right?"*

When the seller restates what they believe they heard the decision maker say then they are communicating that they were listening. And then by performing a listening check, "Is that right?" the seller is asking for confirmation that they have a common understanding with the decision maker about their objection.

Cause: The concept of 'Cause' is used here to suggest probable motivation for continuing to engage with the seller. So in this situation the seller may say something like:

*"But if you don't receive the benefits we've discussed and perpetuate your current condition what impact might that have on your employees, your customers and your company?"*

By offering a proposed motivating Cause the seller is suggesting that the decision maker consider what the long term cost of <u>not</u> making the decision or purchase might be. This again works in concert with the customer's internal buying decision questions, "What could it cost me to make or not make this decision?" and "Do I still perceive enough value to proceed forward with my decision?"

**Commitment:** Ask the customer to move forward with the discussion, exchange of information or decision. If the seller believes that the Cause they suggested is motivating enough then they should ask for the customer's permission to continue.

By the way, this doesn't necessarily mean that the seller should jump right back into doing whatever they were doing before the objection occurred. If the seller feels that the decision maker is not motivated enough to move forward in their decision process, then they may need to have some additional conversation to motivate the customer forward.

A simple example of *Courtesy, Cause and Commitment* used to overcome a logical objection would be:

| | |
|---|---|
| Courtesy | *So you are concerned because you're not quite sure that this is something you really need to have right now... is that right?* |
| Cause | *But if you don't receive the benefits we've discussed and perpetuate your current condition what impact might that have on your employees, your customers and your company?* |

*Kim D. Ward*

| Commitment | *Do you mind if I ask you a couple of questions that might help you to quickly determine whether you really want to do this right now or not?* |

**Important Note:** *Rational Objection Advice - It is recommended that sellers maintain a list of common objections they encounter and then confer with their peers and supervisor to determine what responses might be most effective in different rational objection situations.*

# Managing Emotional Objections

Emotional objections come from emotional distress which can cause decision making to slow and if significant can cause decisions to move backward. The best way to understand how emotional objections arise is to consider the following concept.

*Positive emotions motivate positive behavior while negative emotions motivate negative behavior.*

If customers experience positive emotions, then they are encouraged to move forward in their decision process and negative emotion motivates the opposite. So if asked for a commitment, negative emotions usually elicit a negative response from customers while positive emotions encourage a positive response.

When someone is making a purchase decision and if they want to avoid or eliminate risk, they remain more rational with their decision process. If for some reason the decision maker's sense of risk becomes overwhelming, then they may transition from a positive and rational state of decision making to a more negative emotional state. This negative emotional state might also be explained as a time when the decision maker's perception of risk becomes greater than their perception of expected value in the decision or purchase.

Many sellers have been taught that this "negative emotional state" behavior is a buying decision stall, communication smoke screen or false objection used to cover up the real issues or concerns. As a result, the sellers have tried to handle these emotional objections with logic or rationality. Here is a much better alternative to that approach.

# Three Steps to Managing Emotional Objections

## 1. Identify the cause of the customer's concern.

Emotional objections are a byproduct of overwhelming concern. Sellers should try to identify what or who is negatively influencing the decision maker. It could be that some new information has come to their attention. Maybe someone of authority has caused the decision maker to question the importance or value of making the decision. There are many different influences that can cause customers to become overwhelmingly concerned about moving forward with their decision. In a worst case scenario, if the pain of moving forward in their decision process ever becomes greater than the motivations which are driving the decision then the customer may recoil completely out of the decision making process.

Some recommended questions for identifying the cause of overwhelming customer concern are:

A. I feel that you may have some concerns... can we talk about them?

B. It appears that you might have some concerns about *(the issue or the person)* ... is that right?

C. You seem to be moving in a little different direction than the last time we spoke. Will you share with me why?

D. You appear to be a little less motivated to make this purchase decision at the moment. Has something changed?

## 2. Reduce or reprioritize the cause impact.

Once a seller identifies what has caused their customer to offer an emotional objection then they should try to help the customer to evaluate the possible impact of not moving forward. Sellers should help customers to compare and understand the expected value to be achieved with the purchase versus the cost of no purchase.

Some best practice approaches for helping the customer to weigh the consequences of inaction are:

A. Suggest that the decision maker compare any possible purchase value against the proposed cost of their concern.

B. Question the decision maker to remind them of what it could cost them to not achieve any repairs or improvements you may have uncovered as buying decision motivations or decision criteria.

C. Ask the decision maker if you might assist them in some way with the issue or person who has caused the positive to negative state transition.

Sellers should remember that they are influencers in the customer's buying decision process and have no real authority or leverage other than what the customer allows. Applying pressure to decision makers when they are in a negative emotional state tends to charge their negative emotions making it more difficult to transition them back to a more positive, rational state. But, if the seller can influence the decision maker by helping them to weigh the benefits of action versus the consequences of inaction then they are already assisting them into their transition back to a positive and rational state.

3. Provide information and proof sources to support your influence.

After the decision maker transitions back to a positive, rational state then the seller will most likely need to help them overcome whatever underlying concerns caused their initial emotional transition. Information and proof sources are very useful in justifying purchase decision value. Providing the customer with information that will enhance their understanding of why they are much better off moving forward in their purchase decision can guarantee that the decision maker will not stumble over this particular concern again in the current decision process.

Useful information or proof sources may include:

A. Cost versus benefit analysis.
B. Case studies from similar and successful customers.
C. Reports of the decision maker's employee's purchase motivations.
D. References from satisfied customers.
E. Testimonies from satisfied customers who had similar concerns.

Just keep in mind that when *objections* are presented by the customer it is likely that the decision maker perceives less value and decision motivation than is needed to complete their purchase decision. And yet when *questions* occur it is more likely that the customer perceives reasonable purchase value but needs more information before feeling comfortable enough to rationally more forward in their decision process.

# Negotiations

The idea of *Proactive Negotiation Preparation* was mentioned earlier within the *Presentation Delivery* topic under the sixth bullet point, *Be Proactively Prepared to Negotiate.* There were five suggested negotiation preparation questions which sellers should consider prior to presenting their final recommendations for customer consideration. Here's a little more information about those questions.

## Negotiation Preparation Questions Review:

- ✓ Are you confident that you've done all of the right things?
  *Have you behaved in a truly consultative and differentiated way and have you internalized and followed the Cooperation Selling™ recommendations?*

- ✓ Is there any other value you might guide the customer uncover?
  *Have you asked enough questions and uncovered all of the possible encouraging criteria which might be considered by the customer and added to their decision criteria list? And, have you uncovered a minimum of three ways that you might help the customer improve their situation or condition?*

✓ What could you offer the customer that would improve your position with them?
*Is there anything else you might do for or offer the customer that would further differentiate you and offering? If so, what are those things?*

✓ What concessions are you willing to give in order to complete this sale?
*Are there things which might be considered of high value by the customer which could be used to negotiate other than a discount?*

✓ Do you know what your negotiation top and bottom are?
*Where does the selling price quote start and how low are you willing or allowed to go in order to secure the business and maintain what the company believes is an acceptable margin of profit?*

## High Value – Low Cost Concessions

If sellers are asked the question, "What is the number one thing that customers attempt to negotiate?" without fail they will almost always respond with price. But why price? So many other things could be discussed or considered as negotiation points. Why is it that customers tend to lean in to the negotiation of price so quickly and frequently?

I would suggest that the reason price is the most commonly chosen customer negotiation point is because in that most cases the seller never asked the customer to consider negotiating anything else. Let's consider some other things that could be negotiated. *Keep in mind that these suggestions may vary depending on the selling industry or company.*

Things other than price that might be negotiated:

- ✓ Financing Terms.
- ✓ Delivery Options.
- ✓ Implementation Support.
- ✓ Additional Training.
- ✓ Service and Support.
- ✓ E-Commerce Options.
- ✓ Point of Service Contacts.
- ✓ Productivity Support.

And the list goes on. By the way, it's probably safe to assume that no matter how good a job a seller does helping the customer to perceive decision and purchase value, some decision makers are still going to try and negotiate. So, sellers shouldn't be concerned or afraid of negotiations, instead they should be better prepared for it!

Sellers should be proactively prepared with what I call High Value – Low Cost Concessions. These possible negotiation concessions are items that the seller believes may be of "high value" to the decision maker but are a relatively low cost to the seller.

An example might be a purchased technology which necessitates training for one or more employees in the purchasing company. The providing company may typically suggest that two people in the purchasing company receive training. But might the decision maker perceive extended value in training 5 people instead of just 2? Isn't it possible that with more people trained that productivity might go up faster? And might the customer be less concerned about the purchase price and more interested in generating additional productivity with more trained users? It's possible. But how would the customer know that the number of people in their company who will receive training could be negotiated if the salesperson doesn't suggest it? Here is how that might be approached:

*"Mr. Customer. I understand that you would like to make sure that you are getting the best possible deal with your purchase. But would it be fair to say that if we trained 5 people in your office instead of two that the increased productivity might quickly increase your return on investment creating even more overall value for you?"*

If the seller offers some other negotiable instead of immediately discussing price, then they may find that some of their customers are open to negotiating these other things. Of course some customers will still want to attempt price negotiations. And yet, if other negotiation options are offered then many customers will at least consider the suggested options and some will actually agree to the newly offered negotiation concessions.

## STRATEGY: Prepare to offer High Value – Low Cost concessions.

In order to proactively prepare to offer high value – low cost concessions sellers should consider working through the following preparation exercise.

## Strategy Step One: Create a list of possible concessions.

First create a list of all of the items that might be offered to a customer in lieu of a discount or price reduction. Sellers should try to create as long a list as possible of all of the things they might be willing to give up or give to the customer instead of negotiating price.

*NOTE: If sellers have difficulty figuring out where to begin with this list then they may want to consider things they have given to customers in the past in order to settle unhappy customer issues. Or they may want to review some of the items they have pre-stacked into competitive proposals in an effort to create additional decision criteria weight hoping to competitively differentiate their offerings.*

## Strategy Step Two: Clarify the concessions list.

Once the list is created sellers should not assume that all of the items on their list will make good *high value – low cost concessions*. As a second exercise step, sellers should review all of the items and determine which of them are possibly both the highest possible value to their customer and the lowest possible cost to themselves and their company. These highest value and lower cost concessions are the items recommended for possible negotiation. These concessions can be offered individually or in groups depending on what the seller believes is the best negotiation approach.

*NOTE: One final note about high value – low cost concessions; if the seller offers concessions instead of a discount and the customer is willing to negotiate with these concessions then all is well and good. But if after offering one or more of the possible negotiation concessions, if the customer still wants to negotiate price then the seller should consider removing the concessions from the negotiation table before continuing down the customer's chosen negotiation path. The seller can always negotiate a combination of price reduction and concessions should they choose to.*

# Common Customer Negotiation Tactics

There are currently hundreds of people and companies who offer negotiation training for those who make company purchase decisions. In fact, it's relatively safe to say that as many or more people receive some form of negotiation and purchase training than the number of sellers who receive sales training.

According to people who have attended one or more purchase negotiation training classes one of the highlights for them are the negotiation tactics recommendations they receive in these classes. By becoming familiar with these tactics and reviewing and developing effective strategies to overcome them sellers will be better prepared to obtain critical agreements without adversarial confrontations. The following is a list of the more common negotiation tactics taught in these negotiation training classes.

## Negotiation Tactics Table

| Tactics | Explanations | Examples | Strategies |
|---|---|---|---|
| Influencer Leverage | They say they are agreeable but there are others who will need to be satisfied. | "You know I like you but... we're still going to have to make sure everyone else is satisfied." | Follow DIG Strategies, hold firm, and remind them of previous conversations and agreements. |
| Inadequate Budget | They don't have the money or budget. | "I'd like to... but I just don't have the money." | Hold firm, remind them of previous conversations and agreements. |

| Tactics | Explanations | Examples | Strategies |
|---------|--------------|----------|------------|
| A & B Options | Designed to pressure you into choosing the lesser of two bad choices. | "You need to give us 30% more product or reduce your price by 50%." | Hold firm, remind them of previous conversations and agreements. |
| Convenient Memory | Seems to remember something that never occurred. | "Didn't you say that I'd get free service for 3 months? | Put everything in writing (MOI) |
| Price Vertigo | Seems overly concerned about your quoted price. | "This price seems a little high to me." | Hold firm, remind them of previous conversations and agreements. |
| Higher Authority | Purposefully disempowered them self from making the decision. | "I'll have to run this by my boss and then get back to you." | Follow DIG Strategies. Hold firm. Remind them of previous conversations. |
| Petite Pecking | Asks for several small concessions one at a time. | "You know what I just thought of?" "You know what else I just thought of?" | Make sure all questions and concessions are out before approaching. |
| First and Final Offer | Tries to force a lower price by suggesting no room for negotiation. | "This is all I can do... so take it or leave it." | Hold firm. Restate or question motivating causes and value. |
| Loss Leader | Asks for a larger volume concession, but for a much smaller purchase. | "I'd like to buy 5 units at the 100-unit price." | Hold firm. State logically previous conversations, criteria and pricing. |

| Tactics | Explanations | Examples | Strategies |
|---|---|---|---|
| Balancing Inequity | Gives up a small concession in order to get a much larger one. | "I'll sign a 2-year contract... but you'll have to give me 25% off." | Stay focused on creating a win-win solution. It's O.K. to be profitable. |
| Difference Split | Attempts to split the difference in price after starting way too low. | "You're up here; and I'm down here. Why don't we just split the difference?" | Stay focused on creating a win-win solution. It's O.K. to be profitable. |
| Sympathetic Appeal | Appeals to your better nature and wants you to feel badly for them. | "You seem nice enough. Can't you just take care of me this time?" | Thank them for complements and then share that you're doing the best you can. |
| Competitive Offering | Tries to use the competition information or misinformation as leverage. | "I understand that I can get the same thing from ABC company for 20% less." | Don't fall for this until you've heard it twice. Then decide what you want to do. |
| Magical Misdirection | Attempts to distract you from the bigger picture by giving you a small win. | "I can probably get this approved if you give me a significant discount." | Hold firm, remind them of previous conversations and agreements. |
| Unlikely Request | Asks for something they know you won't do in order to get significant negotiation movement. | "Maybe I could see my way clear to agree... if you give me twice as much for the same price." | Hold firm, remind them of previous conversations and agreements. |

| Tactics | Explanations | Examples | Strategies |
|---------|--------------|----------|------------|
| Shell Game | An illogical request based on logical reasoning. | *"I understand that you need to make money. But, I don't want you to make it on me."* | Restate motivating causes, differentiated value and Cooperation Selling Goals. |

(Note: Any references to DIG (Decision Influence Group) strategies are covered in the Selling To Decision Influence Groups chapter.)

# Information, Applications and Outcomes

As with most educational experiences this book provides the reader with information which they may not have previously possessed. New information is always good for stimulating new ideas and can sometimes help to reshape our perceptions and behavior. But in order for the information to have the best chance of being effectively used, the transition from information to application must occur.

Please consider taking the time to answer the provided questions in order to begin your own information to application transition. These transitions will help to guarantee the fastest and most useful applications and outcomes in your selling career.

*What Information was provided in this chapter that you felt was important and possible useful to you?*

*How might you apply these important points of information?*

*What outcomes do you hope or expect to produce as a result of your application implementations?*

Chapter Nine:

# Implement Agreement

# Decision Influence Step Four: Implement Agreement

In the *Implement Agreement* decision influence step sellers guide decision makers from their *Apply Decisions* to their *Achieve Satisfaction* buying decision step. Sellers should continue using decision leveraging to ensure ultimate and complete customer satisfaction.

Let's review the seller's goals in the *Implement Agreement* Influence step:

- Understand and fulfill all customer decision criteria and expectations.
- Proactively eliminate any delivery and implementation challenges.
- Aid the customer in quantifying expected deliverables and decision criteria.
- Improve ongoing provider and customer relationships.
- Continue to provide "added value" for the customer over the course of the relationship lifecycle.

- Nurture and grow the nature of the business partnership leading to increased customer share.
- Cause the customer to recognize and acknowledge "complete satisfaction."
- Gain extended business opportunities through customer introductions and referrals.

Let's also review the *Influence Questions* (IQ) and customer Internal Questions alignment for the seller's Implement Agreement and the customer's Achieve Satisfaction steps.

| Seller Influence Questions for Implement Agreement | Customer Internal Questions for Achieve Satisfaction |
|---|---|
| • What can I do to ensure smooth implementation success?<br>• What can I do to help the customer achieve complete satisfaction?<br>• Which are the best ways to improve customer relations while continuing to add to our bottom line? | • Am I achieving the results I expected?<br>• Have my expectations changed?<br>• Will I continue to do business with the provider company? |

Many sellers and their companies hope to achieve total customer satisfaction. The actual accomplishment of this great feat is far less common. In Step Four, *Implement Agreement* we will cover how to best reach that goal.

## *Satisfied customers are the foundation on which future business opportunities can be built.*

Business experts understand the measurable positive impact that satisfied customers can have on a company and their success.

If a company can completely satisfy their newly acquired customers, then they stand a good chance of gaining:

A. Increased market share.
B. Repeat business opportunities.
C. Growth potential and "pull through" or "add-on" business.
D. Service and supply business.
E. Prospect referrals and introductions.
F. Superior customer satisfaction ratings.
G. Improved company & salesperson reputation.

Even if a seller guides their customer through the purchase or acquisition steps of their buying decision process, if the customer ever becomes less than completely satisfied, no matter what the reason, then there is little chance that the provider and customer relationship will continue to develop or mature. So it is imperative that sellers positively influence their customers to achieve complete satisfaction with their purchase and that afterwards does what is needed and necessary to nurture and grow complete customer satisfaction.

# Developing Customer Satisfaction

Once the customer has completed their initial purchase, the real work of providing and proving satisfaction begins. There is definitely a relationship between customer satisfaction and the impact it has on customer retention. At this point, customers come full circle with their internal questions when working through their *Achieve Satisfaction* buying decision step. The customer's Achieve Satisfaction buying decision questions are:

✓ Am I achieving the results I expected?
✓ Have my expectations changed?

✓ Will I continue to do business with the provider company?

The customer's answer to these internal questions will determine:

- The customer's residual perceptions of the seller and their company.
- The relationship the customer pursues or allows with the provider.
- Final customer interpretations of the seller's motives and behavior.
- Whether or not the customer will do business with the seller and their company in the future.

# Customer Satisfaction Drivers

INFLUENCE QUESTION (IQ): *What can I do to ensure smooth implementation success?*

INFLUENCE QUESTION (IQ): *What can I do to help the customer achieve complete satisfaction?*

Once the customer completes their initial purchase then the seller may become responsible for completing any required delivery or implementation procedures. In many industries where the seller is responsible for managing customer relationships, they may also become the liaison between their company and the client.

Complete customer satisfaction is achieved and maintained if sellers remember to focus on four basic customer satisfaction drivers and the questions that aid in creating that satisfaction.

# The Four Customer Satisfaction Drivers

1. Developing, bench marking, measuring and managing initial customer expectations
   - What delivery or implementation challenges might be anticipated?
   - What might I proactively do to prevent any challenges from occurring?

2. Executing and Delivering the expected customer experience
   - What might my customer want or need from me or my company going forward?
   - How can I fulfill these needs and improve the relationship?

3. Continued delivery of added-customer value
   - What might be done to deliver added-value as I continue to communicate with the customer?
   - What types of added-value do I think the customer might most appreciate?

4. Measure, analyze and sell
   - What can I do to improve the partnership and provide the best ongoing consulting and support for the customer?
   - What future selling opportunities do I expect to uncover with this customer?

# Satisfaction Driver 1: Developing, bench marking, measuring and managing initial customer expectations

Initial customer satisfaction is based on their expectations for a seamless delivery and the fulfilment of their determined decision criteria.

It is critically important for sellers to make sure that all of the customer's decision criteria are tangible in order to measure the degree to which you are achieving customer satisfaction. Still, there are other challenges that can hinder complete customer satisfaction. Sellers can influence or control some of these satisfaction obstructions while others are a matter of anticipating possible issues and proactively preparing to manage them if they occur.

Some proactive best practices for satisfying customers sooner are:

✓ Keep all promises

Keeping all promises is important if the seller wants the customer to be completely satisfied. The customer has expectations of the seller and company after the sale. They need to know that any promises made or expectations created will be fulfilled.

✓ Effectively communicate the customer's needs and expectations to provider company team members

In many industries it is common to leverage other provider company employees or resources in order to implement customer solutions. Making sure that others (engineers, designers, technicians, etc.) are operationally informed about the customer's needs and expectations will make it easier for them to deliver the most effective outcomes.

✓ **Watch out for and communicate unexpected changes**

Changes happen. Sellers should watch out for and even expect some things to change for the customer between the point of purchase and final implementation. If changes are needed or required in order to completely satisfy the customer, then sellers should try to identify and implement those changes.

✓ **Schedule Progress Updates for keeping customers informed of implementation progress and possible challenges or changes**

If implementing a complex or integrated solution which must be implemented in stages, or if multiple people are involved in the integration process, then it may be a good idea to present the customer with Progress Updates so that they remain informed about the implementation progress.

✓ **Measure initial customer impressions and make necessary adjustments**

Using surveys, questionnaires and social media to measure initial customer impressions provides sellers with real time information about the customer's level of satisfaction. Sellers may use this real time information to make necessary adjustments in order to promote a higher level of customer satisfaction.

## Satisfaction Driver 2: Executing and delivering the expected customer experience

Many customers seem to believe that their providers fall short of their desires or expectations. This most frequently occurs because sellers and their companies are not consistently developing, benchmarking, measuring and managing initial customer expectations. Customers want provider representatives to do five things that they believe will improve their satisfaction levels and relations.

## Five Customer Post Purchase Expectations

### 1. Customers want it to be easy to contact the seller with questions or concerns

Today's technologies have made it easier for customers to reconnect with provider companies to obtain answers, information and assistance when needed. But these same technologies can create communication layers between the seller and their customers after purchase.

Steering customers toward online help sites and applications is certainly a good idea. For many customers the internet provides an acceptable and faster forum to ask for and receive help and information. But at times, many customers still want to be able to talk to their salesperson or service associate. Make it easy for them to do so.

2. Customers want to feel important when communicating with sellers or their company after the purchase.

If customers reach out for help with questions or after purchase issues they would like to feel as important as they did when they were being sold. No one likes to feel that once they've completed their purchase that they are no longer a priority. Yet according to customers, many say that they are made to feel that they are an inconvenience when reaching back for assistance or information after their purchase has been completed.

This is not necessarily the seller's fault. Provider companies may have processes in place for managing customer service. Some of these services may also be automated but also force the customer to go through a series of help menus and/or be placed on hold for an extended period. Should this be the case, then it is likely that the customer will be less than satisfied.

Customers want to feel important after their purchase. Giving them direct access to the seller or appropriate live channels goes a long way to making them feel like someone is listening and that the provider company still cares about them after the sale.

3. Customers don't want to have to repeatedly retell the same story

It is perfectly understandable when a customer calls a provider that they may be transferred to someone better suited or responsible for handling their specific issue. But customers don't want to have to explain their situation and needs repeatedly to different people. To avoid this, create procedures which link customer communicated information, questions, needs or concerns to the next person in the help chain.

One best practice strategy that sellers can implement is to give customers their direct contact information and ask them to reach out to the seller first before resourcing the provider company. If the seller speaks to the customer first, then they can refer them to the appropriate person who can help. Further, the seller can smooth the way by providing the company contact with information they've received from the customer. This prevents the customer from having to repeat their stories multiple times.

## 4. Customers want flexibility when dealing with people, policy or procedure

Most people can relate to the frustration felt when told that they cannot be helped the way they want because "that is not our company policy." Companies create procedures to streamline workflow, proactively eliminate problems and hopefully improve productivity. But those same policies or procedures can be so rigid that they impede customer service.

When customers reach out for information or problem resolution they want to be heard and they want their position to be respected and considered. They want and deserve a reasonable amount of flexibility and should afterwards feel that they have been properly heard and assisted.

In these customer service or help situations it is useful to remember and review the first six *Cooperation Selling – Core Values*:

1. Approach with helping intentions.
2. Change the customer's experience.
3. Demonstrate honesty and credibility.
4. Ask and listen.
5. Be open minded.
6. Create an environment of support.

## 5. When customers have an issue, they want courtesy, information and someone to accept responsibility for their issue

I'm sure you know how frustrating and challenging it can be to talk to a customer about an issue that you did not create and may not have the authority to completely solve. Thousands of employees in customer service roles have communicated that this is a common, recurring and extremely uncomfortable situation.

Let's think about what customers really want when they reach out to a provider company for help. Customers want:

- Reasonable, businesslike and professional courtesy from the person contacted.
- Someone to accept responsibility for helping them to resolve their concern, situation or condition.
- Information that might help them better understand their situation, what has caused it and what might be done to resolve it.

What customers do not want is for the company agent to play the Blame Game. The Blame Game is being told that the person they have contacted didn't cause the problem, is not responsible for the problem or doesn't have the authority to help resolve the issue. There is a simple strategy to maintain credibility with the customer and still follow company procedures for managing the customer's situation.

## STRATEGY: Maintain credibility on a customer service/assistance call.

When customers reach out for help with an issue, question or concern it is recommended that provider agents consider positioning their assistance this way:

*"Mr. Customer, please allow me to accept as much responsibility as possible for this situation. Would that be okay?"*

This best practice strategy does not suggest that the company agent caused the situation nor does it suggest that the agent has the authority to resolve the issue or concern. But what it does suggest is that the person is willing to accept responsibility for helping the customer to move down the resolution path by:

- Providing information.
- Connecting them with those who might be able to aid them.
- Guiding the customer through relevant company processes, procedures or policies.

---

INFLUENCE QUESTION (IQ): *Which are the best ways to improve customer relations while continuing to add to our bottom line?*

---

## Satisfaction Driver 3: Continued delivery of added customer perceived value

The concept of added-value has been a business topic of discussion for many years. The common explanation of added-value is additional or extended value provided by the product, salesperson or provider company which the customer did not necessarily expect to receive.

Every time a seller communicates with a customer after their purchase they should bring with them some additional or unexpected value for the customer. In this way sellers can become a business partner whose contacts are happily welcomed by the customer rather than believing that the seller is only interested in selling them something else.

## Value Adding Best Practices:

✓ Improve the customer experience

If the seller stays connected to the customer after the sale, then can change the customer's expected experience by demonstrating the *Cooperation Selling*™ - *Core Values*. This will positively influence future customer purchases and improve the relationship between the customer and seller.

✓ Respect the customer and their changes

Everything changes. Sellers should look for, expect and respect the changes which take place in their customer's businesses. Change is rarely easy. So if a customer makes changes that can impact what they buy or the way they use their purchase then sellers should manage those changes by finding ways to leverage the changes into the best outcomes for the customer. Here's some good advice:

*Look for change first before offering any new opinions, information or purchase suggestions to existing customers!*

✓ **Always take the high road**

> Sometimes customers do things that sellers either don't like or don't agree with. "Always take the high road" means that regardless of the situation or personal feelings sellers may have, they should always behave with professional demeanor and courtesy remembering to always do what is best for the customer if possible.

✓ **Continue to ask for and create improvement milestones**

> As sellers continue their customer relationships change is inevitable. Monitor the customer's productivity with their purchase. Ask about new goals or objectives and work with customers to aid them in improving their situation and if possible achieve their goals.

✓ **Share best practices**

> Sellers occasionally uncover best practices from their other customers who have created new and more productive ways to use their purchases. Or some new feature or application development may help to improve the customer's ability to increase productivity or outcomes. Whatever the case may be, (as long as it is not proprietary or sensitive information from other customers) sellers should consider sharing any best practices which they feel might be useful to their other customers.

### ✓ Ask for references, referrals and introductions

It continues to surprise me how many sellers still feel uncomfortable asking their customers for references, referrals and introductions. Sellers need to understand that if they don't ask they may be sending the message to their customer that they either don't have confidence in what they have sold or they don't care enough about the customer to also offer assistance to their friends, family and associates.

In addition, asking for referrals and introductions is the best way to survey the customer's current level of satisfaction. Satisfied customers are more likely to give referrals and introductions than those who are not satisfied. If the customer communicates any level of dissatisfaction when asked for a referral, then the seller should interpret that as a signal to find out if there is any way they might improve the customer's situation and perspective. Just remember that:

*Sellers should always want to know how their customer truly feels!*

### ✓ Refer prospects to the customer

If the seller uncovers a business opportunity for one of their customers, then they should consider referring or introducing them. The added value of providing new business opportunities are almost always appreciated by any customer.

### ✓ Remember that relationships require work and communication

Any long term relationship has high and low points. Relationships almost always require commitment, communication and work. If sellers are motivated to develop and maintain trusted advisor relationships with their customers, then they must be willing to put forth the effort it takes to develop and maintain the relationship.

✓ **Use expertise to help the customer with their business in unexpected ways**

Many sellers have experience and information that extends beyond the narrower scope of what they sell. If the opportunity presents, then sellers should share their expertise if they think it might aid the customer in improving their business or situation even if it has nothing to do with what they sell. By the way, the best indicator of whether the customer considers the seller to be a trusted advisor is when they ask for advice about something that has nothing to do with what the seller actually sells.

## Satisfaction Driver 4: Measure, Analyze and Sell

To consistently improve the long-term relationship and partnership with the customer, sellers should measure and analyze customer implementations and success. Sellers should also measure and analyze the customer's perceptions of their overall experience and feedback from any customer contacts and possible future decision influencers. These are called Key Success Indicators or KSI's.

Measuring and analyzing the outcomes produced should be a shared responsibility. There are things the customer can do for themselves to measure, analyze and determine their levels of improvement, return on investment and productivity. But they may or may not be aware of how or what to measure so sellers may need to assist them in identifying opportunities to quantify improvement and achievement. In some cases, the seller may wish to do some of the measurement and analysis. Regardless of who conducts the analysis, it is the best way to prove satisfaction and uncover improvement opportunities.

When it comes to measurement and analysis, sellers should consider the following questions:

- What can be measured to identify product performance outcomes?
- What can be measured that might help better understand the provided purchase successes and challenges?
- How will the customer identify purchase decision success 6 months after the purchase?
- What should be happening along the way at those success milestones?

By answering these questions sellers can begin to develop their measurement and analyzing plans to identify possible improvement opportunities.

Even though the (KSI's) Key Success Indicators may vary from industry to industry there are some natural measurement touch points that may be considered when sellers are attempting to determine what should be measured.

# Identifying Natural Measurement Touch Points:

✓ Time Frame Scope: Does it take more or less time to achieve the desired level of productivity by proposed deadlines?

✓ Human Resources: Have the number of people who must be engaged to achieve the desired productivity levels changed? Has the amount of time they are spending changed?

✓ Cost Benefit Comparison: Has the cost to produce the desired level of productivity changed?

✓ User/Producer Satisfaction: What is the level of satisfaction from those who are actually using the product or service?

✓ Customer Satisfaction: What is the overall level of satisfaction from decision makers and influencers?

✓ Quality of Work: To what degree has the quality of productive work been improved by the purchase?

If sellers use these questions to begin their brainstorming with customers, then they should be able to more quickly determine what measurement areas and milestones will be most useful.

## Ongoing Customer Communications

Ongoing communications responsibilities in the course of customer or account management can vary from industry to industry. It is always recommended that sellers follow the instructions and procedures of their company when determining which responsibilities of ongoing customer contact will be engaged.

Those sellers who are expected to manage the continuing relationship with their customers should consider the following best practice activity recommendations:

- Informal and formal customer account reviews
- Customer service and satisfaction surveys
- Social Media contacts, communications and marketing
- Sharing best practices collected from others
- Informal phone calls, customer visits and text messages
- Hand written notes and information copies
- Invitations to interesting events and networking opportunities

# Conducting Effective Customer Account Reviews

A *Customer Account Review* is supposed to be a *partnership* review. Many sellers, when engaged in an account review, will talk about the promises they have kept or the things they and their company have done for the customer since their last meeting. Sometimes sellers will inform their customer about changes or product improvements that might lead to another selling opportunity. Sellers should also remember that if it is a *partnership* review then they should discuss and review both sides of the partner and relationship equation.

## Recommended Account Review
## Meeting Outline/Agenda:

✓ Commitments kept by both parties *(provider and purchase companies)* since the last meeting. *(Commitments may include Cooperation Commitments, delivery expectations, implementation expectations, service expectations, communications expectations, etc)*

✓ Partnership and relationship benefits for both parties since the last meeting. *(Certainly sellers will be prepared to talk about what they have done for the customer, but will they also be prepared to talk about any value they have received from the partnership. Examples: introductions, referrals, additional selling opportunities, partnership cooperation, etc.)*

✓ Current, new and future goals for both parties. *(The customer's plans and goals are certainly important. But what about the provider's plans and goals? Is there any way that the two parties might work together to improve the odds of both companies becoming more successful and achieving their goals?)*

✓ Changes for both parties. *(Change is a constant force in every company. Discussing what is changing or expected to change in either company may provide the catalyst or ideas for better or prolonged service for the customer.)*

✓ Needed changes for both parties. *(Are there specific changes that either party would like to see made?)*

✓ Successes for both parties. *(Are there any successes that either party experienced as a result of the partnership? Sharing these successes creates goodwill and more appreciation for the other party.)*

✓ Potential improvements from both parties' perspectives. *(Are there any improvements in people, training, process or communication that would increase either partner's ability to better benefit or serve the partnership?)*

✓ Any new information that might help the customer to better use any previous purchases *(Does the seller have any suggestions, information or best practices that might help the customer to derive more value from their purchase or the relationship?)*

✓ Questioning for any new information the customer may have to help sellers serve the customer's needs and partnership. *(Does the customer have any information to share that might aid the seller or their company in providing better service?)*

✓ Any new information that might help the customer to better understand possible future partnering opportunities. *(Is there any new information that the seller would like to share that might shed positive light on any possible future purchase or partnering opportunities? Examples: New product development, future product or service improvements expected, process or communication changes, etc.)*

There are certainly other things that might be covered depending on the seller's industry and the offerings they sell but following this outline will create a solid foundation for the account review meeting and make sure that the customer understands that the relationship is truly a *partnership*.

## Customer Service and Satisfaction Surveys

As it relates to customers sharing their opinion about the seller, their company or any aspect of provided service, "no news" is definitely not "good news." So creating ways to survey customers is recommended.

There are currently several delivery channels designed for customer service and satisfaction surveys. How the customer receives and returns the survey is not nearly as important as providing them with the opportunity to respond. If managed properly, surveys provide the customer with opportunities to make unrestricted comments about their experiences and opinions.

There is an old adage that goes something like, "a satisfied customer might tell two people about their experience but an unhappy customer will definitely tell 8 to 10." I have no idea where this came from or if it has ever really been proven. But my experience tells me that unsatisfied customers will talk more about their unhappy experience and with more people than satisfied customers. With all of that said, there is one thing that we have always known to be true. If the provider doesn't give the customer an opportunity to provide feedback when they are unsatisfied, then they will definitely tell others about their unhappy feelings.

Here are some best practice suggestions for making surveys and questionnaires as productive as possible:

- ✓ Settle on one survey objective (*Decide what point of inquiry is most important and don't dilute the survey in an attempt to question customers about multiple aspects of their total experience. If the question is "How did the customer feel about the service?" then ask service questions. In other words, don't include marketing survey questions. Keep surveys simple and on point.*)

- ✓ Keep the survey short (*According to customers any survey that contains more than about 10 questions is likely to either get short responses or none at all.*)

- ✓ Avoid leading questions (*Instead of asking questions like, "What was your favorite part of the experience?" ask questions like, "How would you rate your overall experience on a scale of 1-5?"*)

- ✓ Avoid using industry terms or jargon (*Customers are less likely to respond openly or completely if they feel confused or unsure about what someone is asking them.*)

✓ Provide customers with the opportunity to elaborate should they choose to. *(Some people feel the need to say more than others. Whether what they have to say is good or bad, a seller and their company should always be interested in hearing what the customer believes is true. Provide customers with the time, space and opportunity to elaborate if they feel the need to do so.)*

# Social Media Contacts, Communications and Marketing

Social Media can be an excellent channel to deliver added value in customer relationships. If sellers want to drive the most value to their customers, there are some best practice recommendations which should be considered. First consider developing a social media communication plan that reflects the answers to the following questions:

- Who should we target?

  Sellers should lean toward social media platforms that allow for personal connection and contact with those decision makers and decision influencers who will have the most influence over future purchase and partnering decisions. LinkedIn is an excellent example of this type platform. At the very least sellers should make sure that they are connected to key decision influencers using the resource as well as the customer company page.

- What should we be communicating?

  In regards to what should be communicated, here are a few best practices:

✓ New product developments, product launches or new service offerings that inform customers of important improvements or changes which might aid them.

✓ Articles of interest that the customer might find informative or useful. Articles can be written by the seller or can be repurposed articles written by others.

✓ Website or Social Media updates which should be shared with customers who might be interested in company or industry changes.

✓ Event invitations to any activity that customers may find useful or gratifying.

✓ Coupons or discounts that are currently being marketed by the seller's company if they align with the seller's marketing plan.

✓ Surveys for obtaining or updating customer opinions and responses about purchases or rendered service.

- When should we communicate?

Sellers should remember that even people who really like them may not want to hear from them every day. Bombarding customers with social media communications could have a less than desired effect if the customer begins to tune out those communications. Sellers should develop a communication contact plan that includes the types of communication as well as the frequency.

## Sharing Collected Best Practices

Most sellers will agree that it is always nice to find out that one of their customers is achieving great value and especially unexpected value from their products or services. Sometimes customers do come up with new or unique ways to use their purchases.

Sellers should share any best practices they may discover their customers are using with other non-competing customers.

# Informal Phone Calls, Customer Visits and Text Messages

Making informal customer contacts with a quick phone call, a brief stop by or a short text message is a good idea. But this type of communication is a *better* idea if the seller makes these contacts part of their overall and ongoing communication plan. Remember staying in touch with customers is important but delivering some level of value to the customer with every contact is more important.

# Hand Written Notes and Information Copies

Never under estimate the power of a hand written note. Whether the seller is sending a simple thank you note to the customer or copying an article or post of interest and then writing a personal message before forwarding it, customers always seem to appreciate the personal touch. Hand written messages or notes communicate to the customer that the seller cares enough about them to take the time and write.

# Invitations to Interesting Events and Networking Opportunities

Inviting customers to interesting events is another way to let your customers know that you consider them a respected partner. These events can be both company sponsored events and industry events that you think might benefit them.

# Information, Applications and Outcomes

As with most educational experiences this book provides the reader with information which they may not have previously possessed. New information is always good for stimulating new ideas and can sometimes help to reshape our perceptions and behavior. But in order for the information to have the best chance of being effectively used, the transition from information to application must occur.

Please consider taking the time to answer the provided questions in order to begin your own information to application transition. These transitions will help to guarantee the fastest and most useful applications and outcomes in your selling career.

*What Information was provided in this chapter that you felt was important and possible useful to you?*

*How might you apply these important points of information?*

*What outcomes do you hope or expect to produce as a result of your application implementations?*

Chapter Ten:

# Selling to Decision Influence Groups

# Selling to Decision Influence Groups: Successfully Navigating Complex Selling

*Decision mistakes occur every day and yet no one really wants to make one!*

How often do you find multiple decision influencers when selling? According to most experienced sellers the answer is most of the time! In fact, the majority of business to business (b2b) sellers suggest that these days they find very few individual decision makers when selling and instead many more *Decision Influence Groups*.

Decision Influence Groups have become more popular in every size business. Although as sellers approach larger businesses the average number of decision influencers may increase.

As the number of decision influencers grows so does the complexity of the purchase decision and sale. This is why understanding and effectively navigating *Decision Influence Groups* is so important.

*Working effectively with more decision influencers increases a seller's competitive win ratio!*

Consider this simple selling example. A seller who makes ten proposals and has two opposing competitors in each selling opportunity might think that if they obtain their fair share of the available business they should sell 33% or 3 to 4 of the proposed accounts. Unfortunately, this is rarely true. In reality, the seller who only meets one buying influencer may easily find that their proposal to win ratio is more likely only a 10 to 15%-win share while those who meet and work with several decision influencers seem to close 40 to 70% of the available business. And, because a seller may not understand why they are not achieving reasonable market share then they frequently assume that the sale was lost to a competitor's lower price.

Because the seller doesn't understand *Decision Influence Group* dynamics their perceptions of the decision criteria, criteria priorities and even the actual desired outcomes are skewed too heavily and toward one influencer's opinions and decision criteria.

So what do sellers need to know and do that will enable them to become more effective with *Decision Influence Groups* and win a larger percentage of the available market share?

## *Changing conditions drive new decision making strategies!*

Any technology industry provides great examples of how conditions and purchase decision strategies are changing. Buyers are aware of the competitive and changing technology landscape and as a result have become more hesitant to make purchase decisions. Their concerns and hesitations are compounded even more with higher priced purchase decisions. No one wants to spend big money just to find out later that what they purchased this month turns out to be obsolete next month.

And yet, most all industries have been effected. There are also other decision hesitation factors which can cause decision makers to become unsure and less assertive when making purchase decisions. A short list of these hesitation factors are:

1. Flatter organizations with fewer managers and leaders.
2. Less available time for decision making.
3. More responsibilities.
4. Lack of specific product, service or solution expertise.
5. More price conscious.
6. Concerns about change.
7. Unsatisfactory previous purchase experiences.
8. Low or no seller or provider trust.

These and other decision dynamics are causing decision makers to be more cautious when making purchase decisions. The underlying motivation for their caution is simple; they sense more risk when making purchase decisions.

## Spreading decision risk and responsibility decreases personal stress and increases effective decision outcomes!

Decision makers today are leveraging the experience, expertise and credibility of others in their organizations to assist them in making better purchase decisions. Whether formal or informal, these are called *Decision Influence Groups*. The size and makeup of this group can depend upon the size and complexity of the purchase and the purchasing company.

Let's begin by defining what a *Decision Influence Group* is and how to identify its members. Then we'll take a closer look at the group's individual influencer goals and motivations. Lastly, we'll review how sellers can more easily influence individual group participants in order to create more critical decision mass and encourage more positive purchase decisions.

# Construction of a Decision Influence Group

*A Decision Influence Group is a formal or informal collection of people who participate in a decision process. These groups are most commonly created because of assumed decision risk or authority delegation for the purposes of limiting decision mistakes and improving overall decision satisfaction.*

The essence of a *Decision Influence Group* is a group of people who are either invited or volunteer to be involved in a particular decision. There are both formally appointed and informally created DIGs *(Decision Influence Groups.)*

An informal DIG is created when the *Crucial Decision Maker* asks for help or information from others because they believe that the information will help them to make their best decision. Informal DIGs are more common when the *Crucial Decision Maker* perceives some decision risk but believes that they have most of the information and experience needed to make an effective decision. Complex purchase decisions can begin as an informal DIG but can become more formal DIG as the cost, scope and perception of risk becomes apparent to the *Crucial Decision Maker.*

A Formal DIG consists of people who have been asked or directed to participate in a more formal decision process because the Crucial Decision Maker believes that by involving others they will increase the chances of a more productive decision outcome.

Some popular reasons for appointing formal *Decision Influence Group* members are:

1. To create the best possible business decision.
2. To leverage someone else's specific expertise into the decision.
3. To increase organizational buy-in, adoption and applications.
4. To decrease personal risk by distributing some of the decision responsibility.

The formal Decision Influence Group is more frequently used when the solution or application decision may require greater levels of organizational buy-in to be effectively implemented. Or someone may be called on to participate when their specific knowledge or expertise is deemed useful to the group.

Whether sellers realize it or not *Decision Influence Groups* have become a decision making standard in the business landscape. As a result, DIGs need to be identified, understood and properly influenced if the purchase decision outcome is to be as productively positive as sellers hope.

## Sellers are often unaware of why they lose a sale to the competition!

We often hear sellers say things like, "I thought everything was fine. But then for no apparent reason the prospect decided to go with the competition!" If sellers do not understand how to identify and navigate *Decision Influence Groups*, then they may never really understand why the sale went to their competition.

## DIG deeper for more effective selling!

The more sellers understand about *Decision Influence Groups*, why they are created, how they influence each other and ultimately make their decisions, the more effective they become in today's marketplace. In essence sellers must DIG deeper for more selling results. Let's examine the makeup of a Decision Influence Group.

# Possible Decision Influence Group Members:

*Crucial Decision Maker:* This is the final or ultimate decision maker. There is normally only one CDM in each Decision Influence Group. The CDM has the highest levels of influence, credibility and authority.

*Decision Group Navigator:* This person could also serve as the CDM or could be assigned by the CDM to manage the decision process or decision information. If not serving as the CDM then the DGN will pass information and recommendations up to the CDM for a final decision. Multiple Decision Group Navigators can be invited or delegated into the group if the Crucial Decision Maker wants to gain organizational collaboration and support for the decision.

*Integration Expert:* This person is engaged to insure that the solution effectively integrates with the organization's current culture, procedures, processes and resources. Because of their specific expertise or knowledge, the IE may also be asked for decision criteria recommendations for reasons of implementation, application or successful return on investment.

*User/Producer:* These are the employees who will use what is purchased. They have information, opinions, previous experience or responsibilities that DIG members feel should be referenced before making a decision. The rationale behind adding User/Producers to the DIG is the expectation that if allowed to participate in the decision these employees will buy into, implement the purchase and hasten the company's return on investment.

*Group Advocate:* The GA believes that they are responsible for protecting the group and in turn act with assumed authority. Supporting influence from the Group Advocate can be vital when creating positive critical decision mass with the influence group.

***External Resource:*** This person is typically outside the natural group; but wants to help the Decision Influence Group. They usually believe that their input is useful and needed. Be aware that their influence may exceed their expertise or capability and that it may not be possible to verify or question either of these.

***Trusted Advisor:*** The TA has high influence and credibility with one or more of the DIG members. Any member of the DIG can be considered by others to be a Trusted Advisor. Sellers also hope to secure this level of trusted relations with DIG Members.

# Decision Influence Group Dynamics

We must first understand that not every possible position in the *Decision Influence Group* requires occupation. As long as two or more people are sharing and leveraging information, experience, expertise and discussion toward a final purchase decision then they are a *Decision Influence Group*. Also, one person can fill more than one DIG position. As an example, if the *Crucial Decision Maker* also possesses specific solution or application knowledge and is intent on using the solution applications personally, then the CDM might also serve as an *Integration Expert* and could also be a *Decision Group Navigator* and ultimately another *User/Producer*.

In addition to the designated roles that someone may play as part of the *Decision Influence Group* anyone in the DIG can be either a *Supporting, Neutral* or *Opposing* Influence on the other DIG members.

*Supporting Influencer:* This person is in favor of a specific seller, perceives the seller's company to be the preferred provider or prefers the sellers recommended offering over other competitive offerings. The *Supporting Influencer* is willing to influence others in their preferred decision direction and share information with the seller that will aid them in influencing others.

*Opposing Influencer:* This individual is not in favor of the seller, the provider company and/or recommended offering. This person will commonly favor either a competitive offering or recommend making no decision *(remaining status quo)*.

# Aligning with Decision Influencers

There is a little known selling concept that can help sellers to best align with and positively influence the DIG member's decision paths.

*The key to navigating the more complex Decision Influence Group sale is creating positive Critical Decision Mass.*

Some sellers have already discovered the importance of identifying decision influencers, aligning with them and guiding them forward in their decision process. They have also learned that the challenge is not really identifying who the decision influencers are. If sellers ask the right questions of the right people then they can usually determine who is influencing the decision, what role they play and how much credibility and influence they have over the other influencers. The challenge is engaging each influencer with meaningful conversation, gaining their trust and support and then guiding them forward in their decision process. When this can be accomplished with the majority of decision influence it is called *Critical Decision Mass*.

In order to accomplish this, sellers must first understand that each member of the *Decision Influence Group* may have their own reasons or motivations for being a supporting, neutral or opposing influencer in the purchase decision. Supporting or opposing any seller in a group decision is really nothing more than a question of personal motivation for any decision influencer. So the real question is what motivates people to choose to be a Supporting or Opposing influence?

## *Decision influencers are motivated to do what they are responsible for and what they believe is best!*

If sellers want to engage and align with decision influencers, then they must understand that in most cases influencers are simply attempting to fulfill their own job responsibilities when participating in a group decision. They prefer to make decisions based on their job responsibilities and how they are critiqued or held accountable in their roles at work.

Once we understand that decision makers and influencers are just trying to do their best to make decisions that will help them in their job then we can easily identify what they want to talk about and what is important to them. Here are two simple examples:

## Example One:

A procurement agent is responsible for securing the best possible price on anything purchased as well as following company operating procedures and guidelines when purchasing. If a seller engages this procurement agent, then we know that they are interested in talking price. Why? Because their job motivates them to talk about and negotiate the purchase price and they want to follow the operating purchasing procedures and guidelines given to them by their company.

## Example Two:

The CEO of a company is responsible for the growth and profitability of their company. If a seller wishes to engage the CEO in meaningful conversation then they had better be talking about helping the CEO grow the company, create competitive advantage in the market place and/or increasing the top and bottom line.

So sellers should engage in different conversations with influencers who have different roles in the same company. Why? Because this is what they want to talk about! It's what each influencer is responsible for at work and whether or not they accomplish those responsibilities that will determined how others judge them. People are motivated to do, and in turn want to talk about what they are responsible for on their job.

Identifying the decision influencer's work responsibilities and decision team roles creates opportunities for sellers to more quickly and effectively engage each influencer. Sellers are much more effective when engaging with this "Job Responsibility" approach as they begin to question and communicate with any decision influencer.

Also keep in mind that the roles influencers might play as part of a Decision Influence Group and their motivations are also extensions of their work responsibilities. Most often it is their work function which causes their natural selection as particular DIG position. For instance, the CEO in many companies is often the

*Crucial Decision Maker* when making significant strategic purchase decisions. This is because the CEO is responsible for corporate strategy, business growth, profitability and innovation.

In order to better understand the finer nuances of the decision influencer's responsibilities and motivations let's take a look at the *Decision Influence Group* roles, distinctive characteristics and each of their most frequently uncovered goals and motivations.

# DIG Roles, Responsibilities, Objectives and Goals

Understanding each *Decision Influence Group* member's roles, responsibilities, objectives and goals will help sellers to align with DIG members and inspire their decision motivation and supporting influence.

Let's review each of the possible *Decision Influence Group* members along with their characteristics, responsibilities, objectives and goals. Pay special attention to the additional notes and insights which follow each of the DIG member explanations. Remember, when discerning the decision criteria and motivations of each DIG member, one person can fill more than one DIG member role and multiple influencers can fill the same role.

## Crucial Decision Maker:

| Characteristics | Responsibilities | Objectives & Goals |
| --- | --- | --- |
| Most likely the owner, President, CEO or other C-Level Executive. Most commonly Tier 1 Decision Level | Final or ultimate decision maker. Normally, only one CDM in each DIG. Responsible for vision, strategy and ROI. | Wants to make the best possible decision in order to support their strategy, goals, ambitions and initiatives. Is generally open to people and information that will serve these purposes. Wants to achieve the highest and fastest return on their investment possible. Usually wants to achieve some vision or purpose. |

*Crucial Decision Makers* have far less patience with sellers than they used to. According to executives they are far more likely to communicate with and trust sellers who possess enough business acumen to understand their business, how business works and is aware of how business strategies and tactics work in the marketplace. Any additional information that a seller might possess which may affect the Crucial Decision Maker's business and/ or organization can be considered a valuable benefit to the CDM.

# Decision Group Navigator:

| Characteristics | Responsibilities | Objectives & Goals |
|---|---|---|
| Executives, Department Heads, Respected Tier 1 or 2 Decision Level influencers. This is someone who has the respect of the right people and as such, has a high level of influence with other DIG Members. | Could be the CDM or could be assigned by CDM to manage the decision process and information. If the CDM then they will make the final decision. If not, then the DGN will pass info and recommendations up for the final decision. | Wants to support the *Crucial Decision Maker.* Looking to maintain credibility and appreciates achieving greater influence though successful relationships and decision making. Comfortable with exerting influence over other DIG members and appreciates a reasonable amount of respect for their authority or position. |

If the Decision Group Navigator is not the Critical Decision Maker, then it is paramount that sellers align themselves with this DIG member role. The Decision Group Navigator will most likely know the mind of the Crucial Decision Maker and will want to make sure that the CDM's objectives and goals are served. This influencer can provide important insight into CDM decision criteria which can be used to create valuable differentiation opportunities in competitive situations. The DGN frequently possesses significant influence over other decision influencers and can override lesser influencers in favor of their own preferences. Next to the CDM, the Decision Group Navigator maintains the most influence and can be vital in creating critical decision mass.

## Integration Expert:

| Characteristics | Responsibilities | Objectives & Goals |
|---|---|---|
| Possesses special expertise, knowledge or experience with the possible solution or providers. Job titles may include IT, HR, Legal, or others who are not the CDM and engaged for advice because of their topical expertise. | Responsible for making sure that the solution effectively integrates. May also be asked for decision criteria suggestions for purposes of implementation, application or successful return on investment. | Prefers to do what they think is the *right or the best.* Tend to appreciate people who respect their position, experience or knowledge. May be sensitive to change or suggestions that are not in line with their current view of the situation or priorities. Likes being considered an expert or integral and important part of the group, company or team. |

The Integration Expert can have far more influence that some sellers realize, especially if the IE also happens to be the *Decision Group Navigator.* One example would be when a company makes a new technology purchase decision. If the offered product, service or solution will need to integrate with any other company hardware, software or processes; and if the CDM determines that the I.T. *(Information Technology)* director who is chosen to serve with the DIG as the IE has enough credibility and influence; then this person might also be asked to serve as the Decision Group Navigator. In this case the seller may find it very difficult to work around the IE for a positive decision outcome. If the IE is also the DGN then the seller must uncover and create decision criteria that the *Integration Expert* will consider high priorities when choosing between competitive offerings. Whether the Integration Expert is the DGN or not, sellers should make sure that their final recommendations are approved by and hopefully supported by the IE.

## User/Producer:

| Characteristics | Responsibilities | Objectives & Goals |
|---|---|---|
| Someone who will most likely use the product or service. If not responsible for one of the more influential member assignments, then they are likely a Tier 2 or 3 Decision Level. | Has information, previous experience or responsibilities that others in the DIG feel should be referenced before making a final decision. | Likes being part of the group and inside the circle of influence. Wants to be of value and/or service. Wants credibility and likes having their opinion appreciated. Most willing to help when the final solution will help them to be more productive or successful. They can't normally say yes to the recommendations or purchase, but they do can possess enough credibility to say no. Ultimately, they like being included and their opinions considered. |

Users-Producers are commonly overlooked as decision influencers by sellers. They can be a previously untapped source of support if properly questioned and leveraged into the decision process. Senior and respected Users-Producers can be engaged by the *Decision Influence Group* when the deliberated product, service or solution will require user buy-in for future applications and ROI. Remember, they may not be the final decision makers but UP's can carry significant influence weight. Few high tier decision makers want to upset the employee applecart so they may go to UP's for insights and buy-in prior to making the final purchase decision.

# Group Advocate:

| Characteristics | Responsibilities | Objectives & Goals |
|---|---|---|
| Believes that they are acting in the best interest of the group. May include screeners, board members, paid consultants or anyone else who acts as if they possess a great enough level of influence and/or authority to speak for the group. They can prefer to keep sellers outside the influence circle. | Could also fill one or more of the other DIG member positions. Believes they are responsible for protecting the group and acts with assumed authority. Supporting influence is often vital in creating *critical decision mass.* | They want to protect the group. They want policies and procedures to be followed. They like it when things go smoothly and as they expected. They prefer to avoid confusion, confrontation and anything or anyone who doesn't follow the rules. They will become assertive if they think the group or members are being misled. They prefer respect for their role and authority. They prefer predictable decision outcomes. |

The Group Advocate is another DIG member to watch out for. The GA can easily become an opposing influence for reasons other than decision criteria. In addition to any considered product, service or solution decision criteria the group may consider important the GA may have additional "operational" criteria which they feel must be provided.

Operational criteria may include things like, the internal corporate decision processes, rules of vender engagement, paper trails, and vender qualification, vetting or validation documents. On the other hand, if a seller can turn the Group Advocate into a supporting influence, this person can be very useful as a procedural guide who helps to complete any corporate required steps, procedures and paperwork.

## External Resource:

| Characteristics | Responsibilities | Objectives & Goals |
|---|---|---|
| Outside, uncompensated influencer. Commonly a friend, relative or outside associate who DIG Members believe are knowledgeable and credible so they are considered useful advice sources. | They want to help. They frequently believe that their information is useful and needed. Be aware that their influence may exceed their expertise or capability. | They want to help. They sometimes shy away from becoming too involved, but once engaged offer what they believe is the best possible advice to those that trust them. They want to feel appreciated for their experience, knowledge, time and efforts. They prefer to have their help, information and advice validated and/or supported. |

Sometimes Decision Influence Group members will reach outside their natural group for information or advice from those who they trust or respect. These people are considered an External Resource. Sellers do not always have ready access to these people for questioning and conversation, but the ER should not be overlooked as a powerful decision influencer.

One of the reasons the ER can be such a dynamic influence is because they have no specific business related agenda in regards to the decision. They simply want to help the decision influencer who asked for their expertise, experience or advice. It is always recommended that seller question all internal DIG members for outside External Resource information and influence. Examples might include, "Have you spoken to anyone outside your company about this decision?" "Is there anyone outside your company who you trust to help you with this decision and who might have some special knowledge, experience or advice?" Remember if sellers don't ask about ERs then they may not find out about them. But don't think that just because you don't hear about them that they do not exist. Listen carefully to what DIG members say about people they have resourced in their decision process and be prepared to ask additional questions about the people and information they might mention.

## Trusted Advisor:

| Characteristics | Responsibilities | Objectives & Goals |
|---|---|---|
| Anyone who is believed by any DIG Member to be a reliable, credible and trustworthy source of information or advice. Must not be perceived as being too self-serving. | Any of the DIG members can be considered by others to be a Trusted Advisor. Sellers also hope to secure this level of relationship with DIG Members. | They want to function as a key contributor to the DIG's decision development process. They want to partner and work with the key influencers of the DIG to create and build value while helping the group to meet or exceed its goals and objectives. |

Any DIG member can become a *Trusted Advisor* to the more influential group members. Sellers hope to become a TA but rarely accomplish the goal because they are so frequently considered by Decision Influence Group members to be self-serving in their comments and suggestions. This does not mean that the seller cannot become a TA. In fact, if the seller does the right things and becomes a Trusted Advisor then future purchase decisions will become much more easily created and attained. (*Refer to the Becoming a Trusted Advisor portion of this chapter.*) Those who do become a TA will occasionally be asked for advice by DIG members about things outside the normal customer-provider relationship. Sellers should be careful to only offer what will be considered to be useful advice.

# Uncovering Decision Influencers

## The easiest way to uncover decision influence... is to look for it!

Over the last two decades I've reviewed thousands of successful and unsuccessful selling opportunities with sellers. One of the more repetitive selling challenges is that sellers do not uncover all of the decision influencers.

The purpose of explaining *Decision Influence Groups* is to help sellers better understand how multiple decision influencers interact, influence each other in the decision process and why. And yet, all of this information and strategy is of little use unless the seller can consistently identify the DIG members. For this reason, sellers may want to consider incorporating the following information as part of their standard relationship development and selling procedure.

Best practices for uncovering all of the possible decision influencers:

✓ Ask your contact(s) questions. Don't make assumptions.

Sellers may assume that because they haven't heard their contact person mention other influencers that there are not any. This is rarely the case these days. In fact, the greater the Crucial Decision Maker's sense of decision risk the more likely they will call on others for advice and assistance when making purchase decisions. Sellers should question everyone they speak to in order to uncover additional Decision Influence Group members.

✓ Ask questions in ways that encourage the most complete and accurate answers.

Sometimes it's not what we ask, but the way we ask it. For example, instead of asking "Is there anyone you have to talk to in order to make this decision?" sellers might consider asking, "Who do you trust to help you make the best possible decision?" Sure, the second question might get the same answers but it is more likely to get more positive and unguarded responses. Sellers should remember to question people the way they would prefer to be questioned. They should pose questions so that the person feels that they care about them, their responsibilities and company. Make it easy for clients to share information.

✓ If the opportunity presents, validate the information obtained from DIG members by asking questions of more than one influencer.

Remember that people know different things and are willing to share different amounts of what they know. Never assume that something shared by one person is all of the information, opinion or insight needed to best guide the *Decision Influence Group* to move forward with their purchase decision.

To uncover all of the possible decision influencers ask questions like:

- What process will you use for making this decision?
- What steps do you normally take when making decisions like this?
- Who do you trust to help you make the best possible decision?
- Are there others who support the initiative? Who are they?
- If you should choose to go forward who might be affected by your decision... and how?
- How do you think others will feel about your decision?
- Are there others who might have input that would help to make your decision easier or better?
- Who might you be helping with this decision?
- Is there anyone who might not want you to make this decision?
- How does _____ get involved when making this kind of decision? (Board members, employees, etc...)

Notice that some of the best practice questions for uncovering decision influencers may also aid in determining those influencers who might be of supporting or opposing influence. Questions like:

- Are there others who support the initiative? Who are they?
- If you should choose to go forward who might be impacted by your decision... and how?
- How do you think others will feel about your decision?
- Is there anyone who might not want you to make this decision?

Some influencer questions may also help determine any internal procedures that may need to be followed if the decision is to move forward. These are questions like:

- What process will you use for making this decision?
- What steps do you normally take when making decisions like this?

These best practice questions are certainly not all of the questions for uncovering possible decision influencers, but they are a great place to start!

# Winning with Decision Influence Groups

## *Information is power when navigating the Decision Influence Group!*

In order to fully leverage *Decision Influence Groups* toward a positive decision outcome, it is imperative that sellers recognize and understand the decision group dynamic.

In a mechanical engine there are numerous individual parts which have been specifically designed to work together cooperatively in order to produce a working engine. Like the engine, *Decision Influence Groups* can also have multiple individual parts. Unlike the engine, they are more frequently unaligned in their abilities, motivations and actions. Still, it is the purpose of the group to come to some cooperative and synergistic decision conclusion.

To suggest that the group cannot come to a decision without the guidance of a seller would be unreasonable. And yet, only by finding ways to inject themselves into the group dynamic can sellers navigate the *Decision Influence Group* and leverage their experience, expertise and motivations into a positive purchase decision outcome. If a seller is to be the most assistance to individual team members and win more group influenced decisions, then there are 4 questions which should be answered with every *Decisions Influence Group* engagement.

## Four important Decision Influence Group engagement questions:

### 1. Who makes up the Decision Influence Group?

Has the seller identified all of the people who will be influencing the decision and each person's role with the group? Consider using the previously suggested *Uncovering Decision Influencers* questions to accomplish this.

### 2. Where is each DIG member in their own decision process?

It is not uncommon for DIG members to be in different places in their own decision processes. One example might be that the *Crucial Decision Maker* perceives strategic value in considering the purchase of a product which they believe may enhance the company's competitive advantage. Because the CDM has discovered reasonable cause or motivation to do a little research into the options and opportunities, the CDM may be in the *Acquire Information* or even the *Assess Options* step of their decision process. At the same time, the Integration Expert or the User/Producer may be comfortable with their current work processes and don't feel a new solution is needed. Both of these DIG members may still be in the Achieve Satisfaction step of their decision process and have not begun to even consider a change or purchase decision.

Where is each DIG member in their decision Process?

According to sellers, one of the greatest challenges they face is finding decision influencers who are significantly out of step with other influencers. Unless someone or some catalyst brings the *Decision Influence Group* members into closer decision process alignment then the odds of the group producing a purchase decision becomes far less likely. In extreme cases where several decision influencers who have substantial influence and credibility are significantly unaligned in their decision processes it may become impossible for the DIG to complete the decision process.

The situation of unaligned decision motivations and decision process steps is a far more frequent occurrence than most sellers realize and can cause several decision making issues for both the seller and the *Decision Influence Group*. This is one reason why the next question is so important.

3. What are DIG member motivational causes and decision criteria?

What sellers need to determine with each uncovered DIG member is why they are in their current decision step. And, if sellers are to guide them move forward in their decision process then they need to know what are each influencer's possible motivations and decision criteria. Only by understanding influencer motivations *(why they want to move forward)* and decision criteria *(what they want to receive and accomplish)* can the seller hope to align with influencers and guide them move through their individual decision process.

## 4. What are the risks involved in making or not making the decision?

For those decision influencers who lack the motivation to move forward with a purchase decision or if they are in the worst case an opposing influence, then sellers need to help these influencers to understand what the cost of not making a decision could be.

Once again, the client's perception of value is generated by their understanding of the cost or pain that might be incurred if they remain status quo. There are certainly risks in making high profile or high impact business purchase decisions. But for every opportunity there is on one side of the decision equation there can be on the other side a challenge, issue or problem. By understanding each decision influencer's perceived decision risks and in turn the possible pain or cost of not making the purchase decision then sellers can begin to positively influence each DIG member forward in their decision process by guiding them to achieve goals and avoid problems.

# Asking Strategic Questions

Once sellers have uncovered the *Decision Influence Group* members then they should consider asking strategic questions to go deeper to gain more influencer insight and information. Asking strategic questions will help sellers discover things like:

- Influencer insights into the local decision culture.
- Details which might be useful in guiding the *Decision Influence Group* to process the decision, generate buy-in, determine applications and increase adoption.
- Short and long-term implementation, outcome and benefit expectations.
- Engaged, prevailing or incumbent competition.
- All of the Influencers decision criteria.
- Influencer perceptions of current and anticipated value.

Some best practice strategic questions are:

✓ What obstacles do you think might exist?
✓ What has been budgeted for this initiative?
✓ What do you think is prompting or driving this initiative?
✓ Where is this decision on your (or your company) priority list?
✓ What would you expect success to look like six months from now?
✓ What should be happening along the way to that success?
✓ What other providers or solutions are being considered?
✓ What has your experience been with (the competition) in the past?
✓ If we could make this easier for you, what would you have us do?
✓ What do you hope this will do for you in the future?

# Creating Supporting Critical Decision Mass

The purpose of understanding the roles, distinctive characteristics, goals and motivations of *Decision Influence Group* members is so that the seller can relate to, influence and guide each DIG member toward their best possible decision.

By gaining insight into what each influencer is attempting to accomplish, the seller can leverage that information into the decision momentum needed to create critical decision mass. *Critical Decision Mass* is the combined influence weight of like-minded influencers who are all motivated toward a decision of consensus.

The more influence and credibility that can be accumulated and applied, the more likely and quickly critical mass will move the decision process in a favorable direction. This is an example of Supporting Critical Decision Mass:

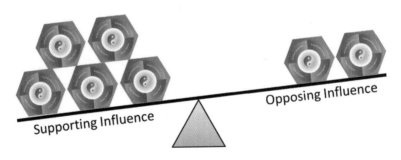

Critical decision mass is really decision momentum which can move in either supporting or opposing directions. The seller's intention with *Decision Influence Groups* should be to create positive or supporting critical decision mass.

In order to create critical decision mass and sell more when working with a *Decision Influence Group* sellers must do 5 things:

1. Identify who might be influencing the decision.
2. Determine or help them determine their decision criteria.
3. Differentiate yourself, your company and your offering.
4. Gain Support Influence with the largest percentage of DIG members.
5. Repurpose Adverse Influence.

Let's consider each of these "must do's" along with some effective questions and strategies for expediting their accomplishment. First, the concept of obtaining, working through and maintaining a single point of contact needs to be replaced with multiple influencer contacts. Consider these best practice strategies and questions for aiding in accomplishing DIG identification, clarification and synergy:

## 1. Identify who might be influencing the decision

The recommended best practice questions were listed previously to help sellers uncover those who may be part of the *Decision Influence Group* under the heading *Uncovering Decision Influencers.*

## 2. Begin guiding DIG members to determine their decision criteria

Sellers should never assume that decision makers or other decision influencers already know what they want or need. They may think that they know all of the needed decision criteria, and yet many do not.

It is possible that they don't have the wealth of information that sellers possess about their offerings that include all of the possible applications and benefits. Might a competitor have helped them develop criteria in an attempt to sell their offering and possibly not what is really best for the customer? Then how can any other seller guarantee and prove satisfaction if they haven't uncovered all of the possible customer tangible decision criteria themselves?

These best practice questions will help sellers to more productively guide customers to develop their decision criteria:

- What would you like to accomplish with this *(product, service or solution)?*
- What specific needs or opportunities do you to hope to take advantage of or fulfill?
- What must occur in order for you to be completely satisfied with your decision?
- What goals do you have and how do you hope this decision will help you accomplish them?
- Why is this decision important to you?
- What impact do you expect the purchase to have on your responsibilities?
- How soon do you need to have the *(product, service or solution)* in place?
- How will you measure the effective application of the *(product, service or solution)?*

Many decision makers and influencers may think that they know what they want until the right seller starts asking some of these questions. In many cases, clients have a general idea of what they would like to accomplish with their decision but they may not have had the differentiated, consultative guidance of a professional and caring seller to flesh out the sketchier initial perceptions. Questioning in order to develop a more complete list of the client's tangible decision criteria, as well as helping them to prioritize their discovered criteria is another great way for sellers to competitively differentiate themselves as a truly consultative seller.

## 3. Differentiate yourself, your company and your offering

Every seller faces competition. In *Cooperation Selling*™ there are several differentiation opportunities, strategies and techniques covered. But remember that sometimes by simply asking the right questions sellers can uncover specific differentiation opportunities that are uniquely specific to the *Decision Influence Group* they have engaged. Asking questions like the ones below, which by the way competitors probably won't ask, is another way for sellers to differentiate themselves.

To uncover differentiation opportunities consider asking these questions:

- Assuming you make a good decision, what could that do for you personally?
- Now that we know what the group wants and needs, what could I/we possibly do to make it easier you?
- Do you expect any personally impacting issues or opportunities to arise as a result of this decision?
- What would you like from a providing partner that you haven't been offered or received in the past?
- Would you be open to additional decision criteria if you found it would help you with more likely or faster goal achievement?
- Would you be opposed to letting me assist you in making the best decision regardless of who you decide to do business with?

- As you look back in the future how will you know this decision was a successful one for you?

We will consider the concept of creating differentiation in more behavioral terms when we outline the *Cooperation Selling-Core Values* in the next chapter. But first let's consider more specific strategies for creating differentiation based on a deeper understanding of individual decision influencers. These strategies and questions will also begin to gain more support from decision influencers.

## 4. Gain Support Influence to create the perception of value and supporting critical decision mass

Remember that support influence is created with one person at a time. Sellers should find out what is important to each influencer and then help them understand how they will help the influencer to receive or achieve what is important to them. By doing so sellers communicate their willingness to identify, focus on and aid the influencer in achieving those things that are important to them. As this is accomplished one influencer at a time sellers begin to create supporting critical decision mass momentum.

### Five Support Influence Creation Strategies:

✓ Start Slowly. Align with the influencer in their decision process.
(*Determine the influencer's motivation and desired decision speed and then stay with them throughout their decision process.*)

✓ Look for clues to understand the member's place in the influence group.

*(What Decision Influence Group role do they play and how much influence and credibility do they have with other influencers?)*

✓ Pay attention to understanding cultural and behavioral differences.
*(People can be very attached to the way they are used to doing things. Become understanding of their culture, behavior and processes.)*

✓ Approach with the helping intentions and inspiration, not defensiveness or desperation.
*(Don't assume that just because you may have had difficulty with a particular Decision Influencer role previously that you will have the same difficulties every time. Don't forget that everyone is different and situations change.)*

✓ Remember to find out what each influencer wants or needs and then simply aid them in doing what is best for them.
*(The easiest way to develop support influence is to simply find out what the influencer wants and needs. Then communicate that you intend to help them to obtain or achieve it!)*

Some best practice questions for creating valuable influencer support and critical decision mass include:

- What could it do for you *(or mean to you)* if you got everything you wanted from this *(decision, product, service or solution)*? Can you expand on that?
- When was the last time that a salesperson suggested that what they really wanted was for you to do what is ultimately best for you?

- Is there anything you need or want from this (*product, service or offering*) that we haven't uncovered or discussed?
- Are there any decision criteria that you know someone else has that we have not discussed or uncovered so far?
- What would it take for you to be completely satisfied with this decision?
- How do you think others will view you if this decision is a success?
- Would a successful decision benefit you in any way we haven't discussed?

## 5. Repurpose opposing influence

Effectively repurposing adverse or opposing influence can be an important part of managing and positively influencing a *Decision Influence Group*. Many sellers have been shut down or lost sales because of opposing influencers. In most cases the seller was either blindsided by an opposing influencer that they didn't know existed or were pushed out because the opposing influencer possessed enough credibility and influence to sway the decision in a competitor's or status quo direction.

In order to resolve the issue or eliminate the problem, sellers must first be aware that opposing influence exists. This is important to remember because many times sellers seem to think that they have a great relationship or big support, only to find out later that they've lost the sale. The underlying cause for this is really not complicated. The issue is that sellers did not obtain a great enough level of support with enough decision influencers and as a result were never informed by other DIG members that the opposing influencer even existed!

The critical thing to remember about opposing Influencers is that they may see no need to confront you directly. They more likely work behind the scenes to influence others in an opposing direction. Please understand that this is rarely an action of malice toward the seller personally. It is more likely an action taken out of a strong belief that the opposing influencer's way is the best way and they prefer to keep their discussions between *Decision Influence Group* members. If sellers are going to find out that a decision influencer is bearing an opposing influence weight on a *Decision Influence Group,* then it is imperative that they have support influencers in their corner.

Another challenge is that many sellers think that they have supporting influence with decision influencers and find out later that they do not. This is why it is critical to confirm support or sponsorship from decision influencers.

The easiest and best way to assess whether someone is a supporting influencer is to ask questions about other members of the *Decision Influence Group.* If the influencer won't provide the seller with information for positively influencing others in the group, then they are not a support influencer. If on the other hand they are willing to share information that will help to influence and sell others in the group, then they probably are a support influencer. Once a seller determines that an opposing influencer exists then they should take appropriate selling action to repurpose the opposing influence.

## Three Repurposing Opposing Influence Strategies:

A. Leverage higher influence supporters.

To leverage higher influence supporters, sellers must gain support from those who are part of the *Decision Influence*

*Group* and also have more authority, credibility or influence than the opposing influencer. This can be tricky and depends a great deal on how much influence or credibility the opposing influencer has with the seller's supporter. Remember, no matter how important a seller becomes to other members of the group the seller is still considered to be an outside source of influence and information to the DIG. So before sellers go to the higher level influencer for help with the opposing influencer they had better be sure that they know what the response will be before asking for assistance.

B.   Create overwhelming critical decision mass.

Creating critical decision mass becomes a viable option for overcoming an opposing influencer when either the final decision is being floated up to a *Crucial Decision Maker* or when it has been made clear that the majority will rule in this decision.

If the seller wants the *Crucial Decision Maker* to override the opposing influencer's recommendations, then it is important to know who the CDM trusts. Does the seller have their confidence and support? If not, the seller had better obtain either direct support from the CDM or the support of other very influential DIG members before attempting this approach to overcome the opposing influencer obstacle.

In the case of majority rule, it would be in the seller's best interest to communicate with any and all support influencers how important it is that the opposing influencer not be made to feel wrong or unimportant because of their dissenting opinion. Remember, when the decision is over and the seller is no longer engaged with the group the current opposing influencer is still going to be there. Don't cause problems for opposing influencers because they may be needed for support with future selling and business opportunities.

Keep the DIG focused on making the best possible decision and encourage your support influencers to take the high road by simply doing what they believe is best for everyone concerned. If a seller uses this approach successfully then they may find that the currently opposing influencer may not be an issue the next time they are engaged with this company.

C. Overcome or repurpose opposing influencers with questions.

Sellers can always ask the opposing influencer more questions either in private or public depending on what they believe is the best approach. These questions should be designed to help the influencer understand that the seller's proposition and advice are in their best interest and in the best interest of the group or company.

These questions are most useful when they focus on one of the following three areas:

✓ Discovering Additional Value

Ask questions to create more perceived value by guiding the opposing influencer to gain a more intense perspective of what it could cost them to not choose your solution.

Refer to *DISCovery* Method questions in Cooperation Selling Step 2 – Refine Criteria

| DISCovery | | |
|---|---|---|
| **D** | Diagnose | Ask questions to help the customer more clearly understand their current condition or situation. |
| **I** | Inform | Share your findings and insights with the customer to determine or confirm perceptions in common. |
| **S** | Suggest | Offer additional recommendations which will improve the customer's condition and create the greatest value. |
| **C** | Confirm | Gain solution to criteria match up agreement while differentiating yourself, solution and company. |

✓ Rational Response Questions

Ask questions to assist the opposing influencer in understanding that based on the total decision criteria of the group that the seller's proposition is the most rational and logical choice.

Example:

- "I'm sure that we can agree that our solution will provide the best possible criteria and goal achievement for the rest of your decision group. However, even though we may fall a little short in one of your criteria areas, wouldn't we still be the best logical choice?"

✓ Higher Road Appeal Questions

Ask for the opposing influencer's commitment to do what is best for their group or company. Remind the opposing influencer that regardless of their personal feelings or opinions that they probably want to do what is best for everyone.

Example:

- "I understand that your decision position is important to you. I believe like you do that the others involved in the decision want to do what is best for everyone. May we take just a few minutes and review why some of your associates feel so strongly about their choices?"

# Becoming a Trusted Advisor

One common seller goal is to become a *Trusted Advisor* in their accounts and business relationships. Even after that status has be achieved with one or more of the *Decision Influence Groups*, the *Trusted Advisor* status can be lost if the seller doesn't do what it takes work to maintain and nurture any relationship. The following are examples of what great *Trusted Advisors* do in order to maintain and grow their status with *Decision Influence Groups*.

## Trusted Advisors:

1. Ask questions and listen before talking.
2. Understand that making decisions isn't always easy so they do their best to anticipate client questions, concerns and needs.
3. Understand the client's point of view, relationships and responsibilities.
4. Take proactive steps to always remain prepared to guide clients in answering their internal questions in order to exceed client expectations.
5. Differentiate themselves with *Cooperation Selling Values & Behaviors*.
6. Do everything they can to understand what the client wants to accomplish and then simply guides and mentors them toward whatever is best for them.

Effectively navigating and leveraging *Decision Influence Groups* is critical to selling success today. By quickly getting higher, wider and deeper in most company relationships sellers can more easily identify decision influencers and produce more supporting critical mass and ultimately... more sales! So, DIG deeper for more sales!

# Information, Applications and Outcomes

As with most educational experiences this book provides the reader with information which they may not have previously possessed. New information is always good for stimulating new ideas and can sometimes help to reshape our perceptions and behavior. But in order for the information to have the best chance of being effectively used, the transition from information to application must occur.

Please consider taking the time to answer the provided questions in order to begin your own information to application transition. These transitions will help to guarantee the fastest and most useful applications and outcomes in your selling career.

*What Information was provided in this chapter that you felt was important and possible useful to you?*

*How might you apply these important points of information?*

*What outcomes do you hope or expect to produce as a result of your application implementations?*

Resource Guide:

# Initiating Cooperation Selling

# Initiating Cooperation Selling

# Getting Started

Now that you understand the *Cooperation Selling*™ process, let's look at how you can adopt it into your day-to-day selling efforts.

*Character is not created by the choices we make, it is revealed!*

As with most things becoming a *Cooperation Selling*™ salesperson begins with a choice. We must choose to break away from traditional selling wisdom. According to many of the top sellers in the world, their selling careers have been built on stretching the boundaries of the sales training and coaching they received in the past and forging new inroads into selling the way they believe is right and best.

If you are also one who chooses to be a top selling producer and one who cares about your customers, then the blueprint for your future success begins in this chapter.

*Every journey begins with first steps!*

Becoming a *Cooperation Selling*™ salesperson begins with focusing on three things.

1.  Cooperation Selling Core Values: *Our values determine our priorities and influence our behavior. Understanding, internalizing and committing to selling values that are aligned*

*with what customers want from sellers is the best place to start.*

2.  Cooperation Selling Commitments: *Have a willingness to make and keep the five Cooperation Selling Commitments so that you can continue to improve your selling behaviors and activities as everything, including your customers, continue to change.*

3.  Cooperation Selling Methodology and Process: *Understand the way people make purchase decisions and then use decision leveraging to guide them through their decision process.*

# Good People Prefer to Do Good Business

*Understanding how customers want to be treated is not difficult once we recognize that they are really just like us!*

Too many well intended sellers have been subjected to generations of manipulative selling strategies and product focused selling advice. I mention this because I've personally encountered thousands of sellers and sales managers who have stated that many of the selling attitudes and strategies they had been taught and expected to use were in their minds unproductive, relationship hindering and in some cases simply wrong.

The byproduct of these ineffective and sometimes inappropriate selling approaches has been fewer healthy customer relationships, commoditized product perceptions and even some adversarial provider-customer interactions. A large percentage of sellers think that the behaviors they are taught to exhibit when selling is not how they prefer to be treated when buying. Also according to many sellers they have learned to behave one way when they are selling and then behave differently in the balance of their life.

No matter how a seller justifies their business behavior, they will fall short of personal satisfaction in any relationship that is grounded in uncaring behaviors and strategies.

## *Selling is really just people talking to people about business!*

Customers eventually recognize when a seller is ill intentioned, unprepared or unprofessionally behaved. Things like honesty, credibility and caring belong in every business relationship as they do in any other. I think that most sellers understand how important honesty and credibility are in their dealings with customers and I want to believe that most of us possess the desire to create a more partnering and productive business relationship whenever possible.

## *Our intentions are revealed by our behavior!*

Customers develop a perception of a seller's values and intentions based on the seller's behavior. Have you ever experienced someone who said that they cared about you but it became painfully obvious that they weren't really listening to you? That is one example of a person's behavior speaking louder than their words.

Customers interpret a seller's true intentions based on the way they behave, not what they say. So if sellers want to make the best possible impression and encourage more customers to trust and work with them, they must make sure that their behavior exhibits the best and most appropriate intentions.

*As our beliefs become thoughts then our thoughts become actions!*

Sellers who want to create and follow the most customer centric selling path should examine their *core selling values* to determine whether or not those values support their customer centric intentions. If the seller aligns their values and intentions with true customer centric selling behavior then their selling outcomes, relationship development and the satisfaction for both parties is greatly improved.

# Cooperation Selling™ - Core Values

To create a truly consultative and mutually beneficial selling approach, sellers should act in concert with what their customers want and expect. To guide sellers on this path there are eight *Cooperation Selling-Core Values* which should be internalized. These *Cooperation Selling*™ values and the resulting behaviors can provide a morally satisfying, powerful and profitable selling platform. These values will also engender a more appreciative, understanding and relationship committed customer.

There are two major benefits to a customer/seller relationship which are grounded in the *Cooperation Selling-Core Values:*

1. Sellers become more confident and comfortable in their selling role.
2. Customers buy more, spend more, remain customers longer and are happier in their buying decision process and the provider-customer relationship.

# The Eight Core Values:

The following is a list of the *Cooperation Selling-Core Values* along with the explanations, possible applications and outcomes that each is likely to produce. I'm sure that you will agree that each *Core Value* is of significant importance when developing customer relationships and completely satisfying them.

1. *Approach with helping intentions*
2. *Change the customer's experience*
3. *Demonstrate honesty and credibility*
4. *Ask and listen*
5. *Be open minded*
6. *Create an environment of support*
7. *Know everything about your solution*
8. *Expect cooperative partnerships*

## Core Value 1: Approach with helping intentions

If we sincerely desire to develop an enduring relationship with a customer, then we must approach the relationship with an attitude of giving and not taking. To approach with helping intentions means that we can best serve our customers, ourselves and ultimately the relationship between us by focusing on the customer's needs and goals, not our own.

By putting our customer focused intentions first we actually increase the customer's motivation to behave cooperatively in their dealings with us. Usually as a result of gaining customer cooperation we sell more, to more customers and with better overall short and long term relationship results.

Truly great consultative sellers have learned that it is always easier and the relationship is more readily accepted by the customer if they approach them with the intention of helping.

## STRATEGY: Improve your customer's situation with knowledge leveraging

Sellers should always approach customers with helping intentions. They should view every customer engagement as an opportunity to leverage their knowledge and experience into some kind of helpful customer benefit. So when you approach your customers ask yourself, *"Knowing what I do, how can I help the customer improve their situation? What's best for the customer and how can I use what I know to help them to achieve this improvement?"*

## Core Value 2: Change the customer's experience

*If you look, sound and behave like other sellers, in the customer's mind you are just like them!*

Over the years many sellers have expressed to me how challenging it can be to have a customer prejudge them based on their experiences with other salespeople. What frustrates them is that prospects seem to judge them as stereotypical sellers before ever really giving them a chance to prove that they are different.

If this has happened to you, have you asked yourself why it happens? You've just met the prospect so certainly they don't know you, your intentions or your selling behavior. So why are so many customers worried, guarded and even sometimes confrontational once they find out that you are a seller?

Customers stereotype sellers due to their past experiences with other sellers who exhibited behaviors that they didn't like or appreciate. In the customer's mind they are simply protecting themselves from a seller who may behave the same as those others who have previously mistreated them!

A single use of a manipulative tactic like *cornering questions* (*"Will Tuesday or Wednesday be better for you?"*) can cause the customer to assume that you are just like those other sellers. So *Cooperation Selling* salespeople must not say or do what others have said or done in the same way. We must change the customer's experience!

Change the experience! It's really quite simple. Sellers must make sure that they don't use any of the same language and/or behavior which have been used by stereotypical salespeople. If you want to change the customer's opinion, then you must change the buying experience! By using the *Cooperation Selling* methodology, language and strategies, sellers can eliminate stereotypical behavior and create true consultative differentiation!

## STRATEGY: Change the customer's experience by behaving and selling differently

We all know how important differentiation is. What many sellers don't know is that by changing the experience they can start to create this important differentiation very early in their customer engagements! If sellers don't talk like those others or act like those others, then in the customer's mind they may not be like those others!

## Core Value 3: Demonstrate honesty and credibility

When customers are asked to sum up the unpleasant experiences they've endured at the hands of those who they consider to be poor sellers they use a lot of unflattering words. The most frequent word buyers use to characterize the sellers they don't care for is... "untrustworthy." In order to better understand why so many customers would use the word "untrustworthy" to describe salespeople let's consider the behaviors that customers think are stereotypical of sellers.

When asked, customers say that sellers have commonly exhibited the following untrustworthy offenses:

A. Broken promises.
B. Misinformation.
C. Missed deadlines.
D. Lies & cheating.
E. Unachieved but promised value.
F. Lack of promised support.
G. Inappropriate, unprofessional and rude behavior.
H. A general lack of professional courtesy and respect.

The good news is that going forward we can change our customer's perceptions of us. If sellers want customers to trust them then they must demonstrate honesty and credibility.

*The word honesty implies a refusal to lie, cheat, steal or deceive in any way; while credibility is the quality or power of instilling belief.*

What sellers must always do is demonstrate through their behavior that they can be trusted in everything they say and do.

Most selling professionals agree that it's important to build rapport with a customer. Most sellers are probably very familiar with several of the traditional rapport building strategies. These include finding some common ground for discussion, talk about the customer's interests or, worst case, talk about the weather.

The truth is that none of these do a great job of creating or building rapport. To make matters worse, customers have heard these same strategies used far too often by sellers who they really didn't like. Sellers have a much better opportunity to create and sustain rapport and build trust with the customer if they'll simply deliver on their promises.

## *True rapport is created by making and keeping agreements!*

Sellers must demonstrate honesty and credibility by remembering to exhibit the following four behaviors:

## Behavior 1: Tell the whole truth about product and service capabilities

Telling the truth about your product and service capabilities will create more sales with fewer unexpected issues after the sale. All sellers at some point face the decision of telling the customer the whole truth and possibly risking their sale or remaining quiet and waiting to see if problems surface later. There is only one best thing to do: Tell the customer the whole truth!

If the customer chooses to go in a different direction, then so be it. But if sellers tell their customer the whole truth and it creates any decision hesitation then the seller can always rebuild, repackage or renegotiate their recommendations. Sellers should never leave a customer with a false impression of their product, service capabilities or company. If they do, then eventually the customer will realize it. It is far better to simply tell the customer the whole truth.

## Behavior 2: Be well planned and prepared

Customers don't want to be approached by a seller who is unplanned or unprepared. Being unprepared can certainly make selling more difficult. But the more important issue caused is the customer's interpretations of the seller's unpreparedness.

According to customers, when a seller is unprepared and unplanned, customers have a more difficult time understanding and tend to believe that the seller is intentionally confusing them. Customers interpret this situation as one where the seller might be taking advantage of them. So if sellers want to appear credible and trustworthy it is important to be well planned and prepared to promote clear and concise communication with the customer.

## Behavior 3: Treat customers with professional respect

Remember the Golden Rule. One seller is not going to do business with everyone. But if they always treat people with professional courtesy and respect then the possibility of doing business with more customers is much greater.

To some degree all customers have their personal expectations of sellers. And sellers never know for sure what a customer's specific expectations of them are until they ask. But we do know that most customers prefer to be treated with professional respect. Besides, not treating people with professional respect will most likely convince them that we're just like the stereotypes they have met and don't trust.

## Behavior 4: Make and keep agreements

Relationships are built on trust. As mentioned earlier, making and keeping agreements is one of the only true ways to build rapport. It is also the foundation on which great relationships are built. Customers must know that they can trust us if they are going to allow us to help them improve their business situation. They must trust us if we want them to answer the questions we ask and open mindedly consider the recommendations we offer. Remember that the foundation of all great relationships is trust!

By consistently demonstrating these four behaviors sellers encourage their customers to understand that they are not stereotypical salespeople. These four behaviors demonstrate the seller's respect for themselves and others.

## Core Value 4: Ask and listen

There has been a plethora of books, articles and training programs written which offer reasons for asking customers questions when selling. Although what seems to have escaped many during the exploration of this topic is the best reason for asking questions.

The three most common traditional reasons cited for asking the customer questions include:

- To gain control of the conversation.
- To better position the prospect to hear our recommendations.
- To engage the customer in the selling process in order to create buy-in.

These reasons for questioning reveal a glaring inconsistency with the basic concept of consultative selling. All of these reasons for questioning are about what is best for the seller and in no way consider what is best for the customer.

*We should ask questions so that we can listen to the answers and determine how we might best <u>assist</u> the customer with their decision!*

Information is the key when unlocking and revealing opportunities to help customers. Asking questions and listening to the answers provides sellers with the information needed to:

- Understand what the customer truly wants and needs.
- Improve the customer's current situation.
- Help the customer make the best possible decision.
- Help the customer do what is going to be best for them.
- Create and offer the most viable and useful recommendations.
- Navigate and satisfy *Decision Influence Groups* by helping them all of the influencers through their individual and then group decision process.

## STRATEGY: Ask questions with consultative motivation

Customers are people. People have needs, concerns and goals. If we ask good questions and then listen carefully to the answers then we stand a much better chance of eventually aiding customers in getting exactly what they want and need! So, sellers should ask and listen.

## Core Value 5: Be open minded

It has been said that, "Minds are like parachutes, they only work when they're open." As funny as that may sound, in reality our minds are always working. The important question is, "What is your mind working on when you are selling?"

From a truly consultative selling perspective at least part of a seller's responsibility is to remain open minded enough to help the customer figure out what might be *their* best decision. Keeping an open selling mind is more difficult when the seller is only focused on selling and not focused on guiding the customer through their decision process.

## A closed selling mind is the result of a misaligned intention!

If a seller's intention remains steadfastly focused on selling something rather than on discovering ways to help the customer, then their mind remains closed to information which could help to improve the customer's situation. By listening carefully to what the customer shares, and keeping their mind open to the best customer focused possibilities, sellers uncover the best opportunities to partner with their customers in their decision.

Also, being open minded and listening carefully to what the customer has to say proves that you care about their thoughts, their situation and their desire to make a decision that is best for them. By keeping an open selling mind sellers creatively uncover even more selling opportunities.

## An open selling mind is the doorway to creativity!

Many sellers are naturally creative. Great sellers are capable of figuring out creative ways to help their customers. We all see things in our own uniquely different way. Enough information combined with an open mind can creatively produce customer options and opportunities that might otherwise be left undiscovered.

## STRATEGY: Find creative ways to help customers do what is best for them

Being opened minded makes selling a process of joining with the right customer in order to creatively design the best solution for them. Sellers should always remain open minded!

## Core Value 6: Create an environment of support

Inadequate service has become so commonplace that, according to customers, they don't actually expect good customer care even if they do have a request or complaint.

But what a wonderful opportunity for *Cooperation Selling* sellers! Because the world seems so upside down in regards to customer service it presents a tremendous opportunity for committed service providing sellers to differentiate themselves from the others. How? By creating an environment of caring customer support! Creating an environment of support for customers is simple if sellers will remember to exhibit these three consultative behaviors:

### A. Partner in responsibility for customer issues and opportunities

This means letting the customer know that you are willing to accept partnering responsibility in achieving their opportunities or solving problems which they believe are important. Sellers should let customers know with questions, statements and behavior that their intention is to help the customer make decisions that will best improve *their* situation.

## B. Ask relevant questions

Asking questions that are relevant to the customer and listening for opportunities to improve their situation is another way to positively differentiate the seller. This also communicates that the seller cares about them, their situation and their purchase decision. Unlike other selling methodologies *Cooperation Selling* encourages sellers to remain in sync with the customer's decision process and look for those opportunities or issues which are important to the *customer*. Asking irrelevant questions or questions that are not logically progressive and conversational will only frustrate customers and convince them once again that either the seller doesn't care about them or that they are not listening.

The best sellers are well prepared with predetermined questions that might help them to discover opportunity. They should have those questions memorized and rehearsed in order to be most consistently effective when they ask them. However, these questions should be asked in a conversational manner.

## STRATEGY: Always ask logically progressive and conversational next questions

## C. Ask the next conversational question

We've all experienced salespeople who were prepared to ask questions but not prepared to have a conversation. Some of these salespeople use what appears to be a machine gun, non-listening and seemingly disconnected approach when questioning. In most cases, these questions are focused on the seller not the customer.

Examples include:

- How many employees do you have?
- What is your annual budget for X?
- When does your fiscal year begin?
- How often do you order X?

Not only are these questions interrogational, they can actually confuse the customer.

Asking the next obvious or logical question makes it easier for the customer to follow the conversation and understand that the seller cares about them and their needs. This selling behavior also enhances the seller's ability to become better informed when helping customers to make decisions. As an example, if as part of your normal selling procedure you might ask a customer a question like:

*"So what challenges are you currently experiencing?"*

Listen carefully to the customer's answer to determine whether you should ask a follow up question in order to better understand their meaning. Let's say the customer responds with:

*"I'm not getting the level of service I want from my current partner."*

Then you should be prepared with a conversational follow-up question such as:

*"Can you tell me more about the type of service you are looking for?"*

This is a logical and progressive follow-up question. The answer to which will give you indicators as to what this customer considers good service.

We must ask rationally progressive and conversationally connecting questions which support the customer's natural decision process if we want them to trust us and allow us to participate in their decision process.

## Core Value 7: Know everything about your solution

All sellers should know everything there is to know about their products or services. They should also be familiar with all of the possible applications, features, functions and benefits that can be obtained with their offerings. What hasn't been unilaterally accepted is the reason or purpose for this knowledge.

*The true purpose of knowing everything about your product or service is to help customers improve their situation by applying your offering.*

Customers expect sellers to be knowledgeable about what they are selling to include knowledge about applications and proposed service. And the most important reason for knowing these things is so that the seller can make customers' purchase decisions easier for them.

Great sellers are vigilant in keeping themselves up to speed and educated on changes and improvements to their offerings. By keeping themselves informed about their products and services sellers proactively prepare to assist customers in making their best choices.

## STRATEGY: Be knowledgeably informed and prepared to better serve your customers

The purpose of being knowledgeably informed is to better serve the customer. There is no need to tell them everything you know, but sellers should be able to share with their customers anything they might want to know that could help them make a great purchase decision.

## Core Value 8: Expect cooperative partnerships

As a *Cooperation Selling* professional, you should always expect cooperative partnerships. If we begin a relationship by expecting a cooperative partnership and we behave in ways that are more likely to encourage a partnership, then cooperative partnerships will more frequently occur.

*"Change the way you think and act toward others and watch how quickly they change the way they think and act toward you!"*
...James Allen – "As A Man Thinketh" - paraphrased

Sellers who completely eliminate the expectation of uncooperative interaction with customers and act in a way that is cooperatively customer centric, will differentiate themselves from many of the selling attitudes of the past. The resulting behaviors encourage customers to view the seller as more cooperative. In return, the customer will behave cooperatively. Change the way you think and act toward others and watch how quickly they change the way they think and act toward you.

STRATEGY: Earn cooperative partnerships with partnership expectations and behavior

Expect cooperative partnerships. Then behave in ways that create these partnerships and the outcome will most likely be that you enjoy more cooperative partnerships!

## Core Values - Conclusions

Internalizing and exhibiting these *Cooperation Selling – Core Values* can make a tremendous difference when your intention is to develop cooperative, meaningful and mutually beneficial customer relationships.

*Just because something has always been done a certain way doesn't make it right, it only makes it common!*

Just because the buying and selling relationship has been sometimes viewed by both parties as somewhat adversarial doesn't mean that these perceptions must continue. If sellers can change the way they think and feel about their professional selling role and their prospective customer partners, then I contend that the resulting cooperative, profitable and time enduring relationships created are worth the effort.

# Cooperation Selling™ - Commitments

For sellers to be most effective in today's hyper-competitive business environment and in order to reach the higher echelons of customer-centric professionalism it takes commitment. The greatest sellers never view selling as simply a job. They love to do it! And they commit to doing it the very best that they can! Great sellers also believe that the way they sell is just as important as how much they sell!

*Anyone who has ever been truly great at anything started and succeeded with commitment!*

In order to stay true to the purpose of customer-centric selling there are five *Cooperation Selling*™ *Commitments* that great sellers feel are important. Only by focusing on what is best for our customers and then consistently monitoring and measuring our work for performance improvement opportunities can we achieve the highest possible levels of success as true *Cooperation Selling*™ professionals.

# Five Cooperation Selling Commitments

Great sellers view selling as a profession which requires the same high levels of commitment, evaluation, continuing education and consistent improvement as any other well respected profession. Some of them may have begun their selling careers with natural talent or ability but the truly great sellers who create for themselves lifelong careers know that being fortunate enough to have some natural selling ability is just a starting point.

A great selling career requires a commitment to continuous improvement if the seller is to reach and maintain peak professionalism and performance. There are many personal selling commitments which have been uncovered from top sellers over the years. If we simply review a distillation of the commitments here are the top five:

## Commitment 1: I must study and understand how people make decisions.

If we truly care about our customers then we must do our best to understand why they think the way they do, what process they use for making decisions and their motivations for making them. Only by understanding how people make decisions can we partner with them and accompany them through their decision process.

## Commitment 2: I must use a selling process which encourages customers to allow me to accompany and guide them toward their best decisions.

Sellers should use behaviors and communications that convince customers that they care enough to expertly inform and guide them toward their best purchase decisions. They should use a selling process that eliminates customer apprehension, fear and regret while creating instead a working relationship of harmony, trust and cooperation. A high priority seller's goal should be to encourage all of their customers to become quickly comfortable with leveraging the seller's expertise into their buying decision process.

## Commitment 3: I must record and quantify my selling behaviors and activities so I can continually measure my abilities, improvement areas and successes.

Sellers should be honest with themselves. Only by recording, tracking and trending behaviors, activities and results can they develop a true picture of their abilities and effectiveness in any selling responsibility. Sellers need real time information if they are going to serve their marketplace effectively and be most successful at selling. The work information that they record and quantify provides them with the special insights they need to determine if they are being effective and if their customers are receptive to their process, intentions and abilities.

## Commitment 4: I must continually strive for improvement in my work and in myself.

A commitment to continuous improvement creates a foundation of greatness in any chosen endeavor. This concept should extend beyond the volume of sales that sellers produce. It should also extend to their personal commitment to improve themselves and their selling abilities.

## Commitment 5: I must always behave like a professional adult.

Customers respect and appreciate business people who respect themselves and others. Acting like a professional adult in all business and selling situations pays huge trust and relationship dividends over time with any customer.